THE THIRD REICH OF DREAMS

THE THIRD REICH OF DREAMS

THE NIGHTMARES OF A NATION

CHARLOTTE BERADT

TRANSLATED BY DAMION SEARLS
FOREWORD BY DUNYA MIKHAIL

PRINCETON UNIVERSITY PRESS

PRINCETON *&* OXFORD

MIX
Paper | Supporting responsible forestry
FSC www.fsc.org   FSC® C008955

First published as *Das Dritte Reich des Traums* by Charlotte Beradt, Nymphenburger Verlagshandlung GmbH, Munich, 1966.

Copyright © 1966 by Charlotte Beradt

This edition is published by arrangement with Amanda Rubin and Robin Shohet

English translation copyright © 2025 by Damion Searls

Foreword copyright © 2025 by Dunya Mikhail

Published by Princeton University Press
41 William Street, Princeton, New Jersey 08540
99 Banbury Road, Oxford OX2 6JX

press.princeton.edu

ISBN 978-0-691-24351-1
ISBN (e-book) 978-0-691-24352-8

British Library Cataloging-in-Publication Data is available

Editorial: Priya Nelson and Emma Wagh
Production Editorial: Jenny Wolkowicki
Jacket design: Katie Osborne
Production: Danielle Amatucci
Publicity: Tyler Hubbert and Kate Farquhar-Thomson

Jacket image: MaYcaL / iStock

This book has been composed in Arno and Gamay

Printed in the United States of America

10 9 8 7 6 5 4 3 2 1

CONTENTS

FOREWORD
BY DUNYA MIKHAIL

Charlotte Beradt, a progressive journalist in Berlin, wakes up one morning to the unsettling reality of Hitler's ascent to power. Not long after that 30th day of January 1933, she finds herself in the grip of a harrowing nightmare. Drenched in sweat, teeth clenched, she struggles to shake off the horrors that plagued her sleep—chased, shot at, tortured, scalped. Night after night, these tormenting dreams persist until a thought dawns on her: She must not be alone. The dreams that filled her nights must fill the nights of others in these dark times. So Beradt begins to collect dreams from trusted neighbors and friends, documenting the dreamscapes induced by the regime as compelling evidence of its tyranny.

This task proved challenging. Many people were fearful of sharing their dreams. Beradt recounts several instances of individuals dreaming that dreams themselves were outlawed (but they dreamed anyway). A woman confided that, in her dream, the police used a mind-reading device. As her favorite opera *The Magic Flute* crescendoed to the line "That is the devil, certainly," she found herself ensnared. The authorities detected that she thought of Hitler as the devil. Another dreamer, a twenty-two-year-old woman with a delicately shaped but noticeably curved nose, thought everyone assumed she was Jewish. Her dreams were full of noses and identity papers, then "suddenly there was a scream: They're coming! Everyone there knew who 'they' were and what our crime was. Run, run away! I went looking for a high-up hiding place—up in the trees? on top of a cupboard in the restaurant? Suddenly I was lying at the bottom of a big pile of dead bodies, I didn't know how they got there, but at last I'd found a good hiding place."

Four weeks after Hitler took power, Beradt faced a publishing ban on her work and, amid the sweeping crackdown on Communists after the Reichstag Fire Decree, endured arrest alongside her husband, Heinz Pol. Once released, Beradt secretly resumed her task of gathering dreams from her fellow Germans, Jews and non-Jews. She refrained from revealing her purpose because she wanted their answers to be as unembellished as possible. Over a period of six years, she gathered around three hundred dreams—windows into the soul of a nation in turmoil.

The Nazis viewed intellectuals, writers, and journalists as threats to their system. Many liberal writers, like Beradt, were seen as obstacles to the dissemination of Nazi ideology, and were thus targeted for harassment, arrest, and imprisonment. Beradt's seminal work stands as a powerful testament to one such moment in history, with profound insights that can be gleaned from the dreams of those who lived through it. Witnessing firsthand the erosion of democratic freedoms and the systematic persecution of minority groups, Beradt became increasingly alarmed by the rapid descent into dictatorship, and the chilling ways these dreams mirrored, anticipated, or even enacted Nazi terror. Ranging from the surreal to the hauntingly familiar, they offer a glimpse into the subconscious of a nation under totalitarianism, where even the most intimate thoughts are subject to scrutiny.

In Kafka's story "The Metamorphosis," the protagonist Gregor Samsa awakens one morning to find himself transformed into a monstrous vermin, a terrifying metamorphosis that leaves him alienated and rejected by his family. So too Nazi ideology, with racial exclusion at its core, rendered large segments of the German population unworthy of belonging, almost overnight. Jews and political opponents found themselves systematically dehumanized, isolated, and eventually exterminated. The metamorphosis of Germany into a totalitarian state involved the comprehensive dismantling of democratic institutions, granting Hitler and the Nazis unchecked powers. Like Gregor, suddenly powerless to escape his new form, the German people found themselves trapped. The Gestapo, propaganda, and a pervasive climate of fear ensured compliance, reinforcing the new order. In both Kafka's tale and historical reality, the transformation was not just physical but psychological and social. As a nation, Germany under Nazi rule underwent profound moral decay, embracing policies that led to unfathomable atrocities. Gregor's fate— loneliness, degradation, and death—is mirrored in the destruction brought upon Germany, its citizens, and its victims.

Beradt, in her analysis of a woman's dream in which "the tiled stove in her living room has become an agent of terrorism," uses a quote from George Orwell as an epigraph: "There was of course no way of knowing whether you were being watched at any given moment . . . It was even conceivable that they watched everybody all the time . . . You had to live—did live, from habit that became instinct—in the assumption that every sound you made was overheard, and, except in darkness, every move scrutinized." She points out that "Orwell's Big Brother didn't exist yet" at the time these dream accounts were recorded. But Orwell's words highlight the pervasive fear and surveillance that characterized the era she was documenting, even before the Orwellian vision of totalitarian surveillance became widely recognized.

I still vividly recall the first time I delved into Orwell's novel *1984* while studying at the University of Baghdad. The oppressive atmosphere of the novel resonated with me due to its similarities with the situation in Iraq at that time, making Big Brother's ever-watchful eye feel all too real. Propaganda and manipulation of truth were used to control society. The "thought police" turned citizens against each other through fear. Children were encouraged to report on their parents, and writers were incentivized to spy on one another, creating a society where trust was virtually nonexistent.

As a poet who has navigated the treacherous terrain of dictatorship and censorship, I encounter Beradt's experience during Hitler's time, when fear and suspicion permeated society, with the same profound sense of recognition. I am reminded of my own experience marked by the relentless pursuit of truth amidst the chaos of war. I often relied on metaphors in my writing and communication with friends. It was common practice to replace words with other, safer words. When I left my country (in the mid-1990s), I wrote a letter to a friend in Baghdad. I asked her how "the flowers in her garden" were doing. She replied that "they are withering," to mean the situation in the country was becoming even worse. My personal library which I left behind included banned books that I hid inside the covers of unbanned books. Similarly, Beradt coded the dreams she collected and hid them inside bookbindings in her personal library. She replaced the word "Party" with "family" and the word "arrest" with "flu"; she called Hitler "Uncle Hans." Eventually, Beradt smuggled that subversive archive of dreams out of the country. She sent it to friends abroad as book burnings and home searches became routine under Nazi control. As a Jewish woman and opponent of the Nazi regime, Beradt knew she would have to leave her country. Her husband, Heinz Pol, who had worked for the *Vossische Zeitung*, Germany's foremost liberal newspaper, quickly fled to Prague. In 1938, she married the writer and lawyer Martin Beradt. Both fled to London in 1939 and arrived in New York in 1940, where they joined a community of fellow exiles, including intellectuals Hannah Arendt and Heinrich Blücher. Beradt worked as a hairdresser to support herself and her husband. After the war, she returned to her literary pursuits, which included translating Hannah Arendt's essays from English into German and *The Third Reich of Dreams*, which was first published in Germany in 1966 after the retrieval of her transcripts.

The book's eleven chapters feature approximately seventy-five dreams. Each chapter is given an evocative title that captures the essence of the dreams that follow, guided by epigraphs from profound thinkers like T. S. Eliot, Hannah Arendt, Brecht, Orwell, and Kafka. The dream narratives are enriched by Beradt's unadorned commentary. Her insights draw from a clear understanding shaped by the harsh realities she faced, lending a unique depth to her observations. She masterfully intertwines her personal history with the dreams she shares, offering readers a poignant glimpse into the era's oppressive atmosphere and the psychological toll it took on those who lived through it. Her sharp commentary provides a critical lens that not only deepens the understanding of each account but also reveals the broader social and political undercurrents of the time.

Rather than treating dreams as mere backgrounds within a conventional historical record, Beradt prioritized their fantastical narrative. In doing so, she transformed dreams from passive reflections of reality into active, dynamic narratives that reveal the deeper emotional and psychological currents of society. Thus she recognized the intrinsic value of dreams as conduits of deeper truths whose symbols often resonate more powerfully than any analytical interpretation. Through insightful reflections on the dreams, Beradt delves into the complex interplay between dreams and reality, shedding light on the ways in which individual psyches were shaped by the broader currents of political ideology and societal norms.

These dreams qualify as poems, though unintentional and unedited poems written by citizens in their sleep—a realm where the repositories of desires, fears, and aspirations are often connected to the waking reality. Beradt's argument that these dreams are "beyond interpretation" emphasizes her perspective of these dreams as reflections of waking life rather than cryptic symbols needing interpretation. In her view, dreams do not disguise but rather reveal. In poetry, metaphors can open up layers of meaning and resonance that enrich the readers' experiences, making them reflect and feel rather than just understand. In these dreams, the same principles apply, though perhaps more raw and unfiltered. The dreams Beradt collected, unshaped by the conscious mind's intent to create art, nonetheless function as poignant, uncensored expressions of the subconscious. They act as direct windows into the inner lives of the individuals who dreamed them, mirroring the societal pressures and fears that were omnipresent. They are not merely to be decoded like puzzles, but are to be experienced as stark representations of the dreamers' lived experiences and the societal context that shaped those experiences. This is similar to how poetry often works (at least in my opinion); it doesn't always seek to obscure but to illuminate, evoke, and provoke. In this way, these dreams encapsulate raw emotions and realities, presented not through deliberate poetic devices but through the spontaneous production of the sleeping psyche. Each dream, like a poem, carries its own imagery and internal tension, resonating with the collective experiences of an era marked by its own scars and truths.

Revisiting this book today is essential not only because it's a groundbreaking work but because it's incredibly timely. As we observe resonances in today's landscape of racism, propaganda, and the penchant for surveillance, Beradt's observations become strikingly relevant. The book reveals how the oppressive forces of dictatorship infiltrated what is typically regarded as the most private realm of the individual—dreams. This exploration is not just a historical inquiry but a stark warning about the enduring nature of totalitarian tactics and their ability to permeate even our most intimate thoughts and fears. In an era where personal freedoms are increasingly under threat, Beradt's meticulous documentation of dreams under the Nazi regime stands as a testament to the importance of preserving the sanctity of our human dignity against oppressive political systems.

Beradt references a statement by Robert Ley, a high-ranking Nazi official, quoted in Hannah Arendt's *The Origins of Totalitarianism*, that claims the only private individual left in Germany is the one who is asleep. However, Beradt's book dispels this notion, illustrating how even sleep, which should offer refuge, was not immune to the encroachment of Nazi ideology. Instead, dreams became a vivid battleground where the psychological effects of the regime's propaganda and intimidation seeped in, erasing the sanctity and autonomy of the private self. In many cases, it was precisely during sleep that the anxieties, fears, and oppressive control of the state stripped individuals of their private identities, revealing the far-reaching grasp of totalitarianism. This is a poignant reminder that the battle for freedom is waged not only in the streets but also in the recesses of the mind. In documenting the dreams of the oppressed, Beradt beckons us to recognize the profound impact of authoritarian rule on the psyche, where fear and control permeate even the subconscious. Through these dreams that slip through the cracks of history to resurface in the breaths of the night, she highlights the pervasive reach of totalitarian regimes, compelling us to remain vigilant against tyranny in all its forms and protect the sanctity of free thought.

This book made me realize that our dreams speak volumes about the world we inhabit. When the weight of oppression bears down upon us, our dreams adapt, reflecting the struggle for survival and the yearning for immediate relief. These dreams unfold horizontally in our slumbering, navigating the labyrinth of our present challenges, seeking cracks and crevices through which we might slip free from the grip of tyranny. The horizontal trajectory of our dreams mirrors the constriction of our reality, confined by the walls of our circumstances and the shadows of our fears. Conversely, in times of peace and stability, the canvas of our dreams broadens, and our aspirations take a vertical leap. Freed from the shackles of mere survival, our minds ascend to the lofty realms of possibility, innovation, and growth. We dare to envision futures that extend beyond the horizon, driven by the boundless opportunities before us. These vertical dreams are not just about escaping the present but about transforming it, building upon it to reach unprecedented heights. The nature of our dreams, whether they sprawl outward or climb upward, serves as a reflection of the world around us.

Tell me how you dream, and I will tell you about the world you live in.

Dunya Mikhail

THE THIRD REICH OF DREAMS

CHAPTER ONE

HOW THIS BOOK CAME TO BE

In a dream, in a vision of the night,
when deep sleep falls upon men, in slumberings upon the bed;
then he opens the ears of men,
and seals their instruction.

—JOB

The only private individuals left in Germany are people
sleeping.

—ROBERT LEY, NAZI HEAD OF THE GERMAN
LABOR FRONT

Three days after Hitler seized power, Mr. S., about sixty years old, the owner of a mid-sized factory, had a dream in which no one touched him physically and yet he was broken. This short dream depicted the nature and effects of totalitarian domination as numerous studies by political scientists, sociologists, and doctors would later define them, and did so more subtly and precisely than Mr. S. would ever have been able to do while awake. This was his dream:

> Goebbels came to my factory. He had all the employees line up in two rows, left and right, and I had to stand between the rows and give a Nazi salute. It took me half an hour to get my arm raised, millimeter by millimeter. Goebbels watched my efforts like a play, without any sign of appreciation or displeasure, but when I finally had my arm up, he spoke five words: "I don't want your salute." Then he turned around and walked to the door. So there I was in my own factory, among my own people, pilloried with my arm raised. The only way I was physically able to keep standing there was by fixing my eyes on his clubfoot as he limped out. I stood like that until I woke up.

Mr. S. was a self-confident, honest and upright man, almost a little dictatorial. His factory had been the most important thing to him throughout his long life. As a Social Democrat, he had employed many of his old Party comrades over the past twenty years. It is fair to say that what happened to him in his dream was a kind of psychological torture, as I spontaneously called it

3

when he told me his dream in 1933, a few weeks after he'd had it. Now, though, in hindsight, we can also find in the dream—expressed in images of uncanny, sleepwalkerish clarity—themes of alienation, uprooting, isolation, loss of identity, a radical break in the continuity of one's life: concepts that have been widely popularized, and, at the same time, widely mythologized. This man had to dishonor and debase himself in the factory that was practically his whole sense of self, and do so in front of employees representing his lifelong political views—the very people over whom he is a paternalistic authority figure, with this sense of authority being the most powerful component of who he feels he is as a person. Such humiliation ripped the roots up out of the soil he had made his own, robbed him of his identity, and completely disoriented him; he felt alienated not only from the realities of his life but from his own character, which no longer felt authentic to him.

Here we have a man who dreamed of political and psychological phenomena drawn directly from real life—a few days after a current political event, the so-called "seizure of power." He dreamed about these phenomena so accurately that the dream captured the two forms of alienation so often equated or confused with each other: alienation from the environment and alienation from oneself. And he came to an accurate conclusion: that his attempt in front of everyone to toe the Nazi line,[1] his public humiliation, ended up being nothing but a rite of passage into a new world of totalitarian power—a political maneuver, a cold and cynical human experiment in applying state power to break the individual's will. The fact that the factory owner crumbled without resistance, but also without his downfall having any purpose or meaning, makes his dream a perfect parable for the creation of the submissive totalitarian subject. By the time he stands there at the end of the dream, unable to lower his arm again now that he's finally raised it, staring at Goebbels's clubfoot in petty revenge against the man who holds all the true power and only in that way managing to stay on his own two feet at all, his selfhood has been methodically demolished with the most up-to-date methods, like an old-fashioned house that has to make way for the new order. And yet what has happened to him, while sad, is hardly a tragedy—it even has something of a farce about it. The dream depicts not so much an individual's fate as a typical event in the process of transformation. He has not even become unheroic, much less an anti-hero—he has become a non-person.

This dream kept its grip on Mr. S. and recurred many times, always with new humiliating details. "Sweat ran down my face as I struggled to raise my arm, and it looked like tears, like I was crying in front of Goebbels." Or: "I looked at my workers' faces, in search of sympathy or reassurance, but the faces didn't even show scorn or contempt—they were empty." On one occasion, the dream expressed its message with devastating clarity, dumbed down to the most obvious level: During the half-hour struggle to raise his arm, his spine broke.

None of this should be taken to mean that Mr. S.'s dream made him a broken man in real life, or, in the other direction, that he had these dreams because he was broken. While suffering somewhat under the regime, he remained free, in relatively good spirits, and encountered no particular difficulties in his business for a long time. But the dream left a deep impression on him—"left its mark" on him, as he put it. When he told me his dream, during a discussion of politics, his face turned red and his voice shook. Even though it recurred, this dream should not be seen as a retreat into the pathological world of obsessive thoughts; it expressed the real compulsion and coercion going on around him, and even if he may not have understood the underlying nature of these circumstances, he picked up on it and logically thought it through in his dream.

Paul Tillich, the philosopher and theologian, had the same kind of dream for months after leaving Germany in 1933 and testified to its nature and effects on the dreamer: "For months I dreamed about [the experience of Nazism], literally, and woke with the feeling that our existence was being changed. In my conscious time I felt that we could escape the worst, but my subconscious knew better."[2]

The factory owner's dream—what should we call it? "The Dream of the Raised Arm"? "The Dream of Remaking the Individual"?—seemed to have come directly from the same workshop where the totalitarian regime was putting together the mechanisms by which it would function overall. It confirmed an idea I had already had in passing: that dreams like this should be preserved for posterity. They might serve as evidence, if the Nazi regime as a historical phenomenon should ever be brought to trial, for they seemed full of information about people's emotions, feelings, and motives while they were being turned into cogs of the totalitarian machine. Someone who sits down to keep a diary does so intentionally, and shapes, clarifies, and obscures the material in the process. Dreams of this kind, in contrast—not diaries but nightaries, you might say[3]—emerge from involuntary psychic activity, even as they trace the internal effects of external political events as minutely as a seismograph. Thus dream images might help interpret the structure of a reality about to turn into a nightmare.

And so I began to collect the dreams that the Nazi dictatorship had as it were dictated. It was not entirely an easy matter, since more than a few people were nervous about telling me their dreams; I even ran across the dream "It's forbidden to dream but I'm dreaming anyway" a half dozen times in almost identical form.

I asked the people I came into contact with about their dreams; I didn't have much access to enthusiastic supporters of the regime, or people benefiting from it, and their internal reactions in this context would in any case not have been particularly useful. I asked the dressmaker, the neighbor, an aunt, a milkman, a friend, almost always without revealing my purpose since I wanted their answers to be as unembellished as possible. More than once, their lips were unsealed after I told them my factory owner's dream as an example. Several had been through something similar themselves: dreams about current political events that they had immediately understood and that had made a deep impression on them. Other people were more naïve and not entirely clear on the meaning of their dreams. Naturally, each dreamer's level of understanding and ability to retell their dreams depended on their intelligence and education. Still, whether young lady or old man, manual laborer or professor, however good or bad their memory or expressive ability, all had dreams containing aspects of the relationship between the totalitarian regime and the individual that had not yet been academically formulated, like the elements of "crushing someone's personhood" in the factory owner's dream.

It goes without saying that all these dream images were sometimes touched up by the dreamer, consciously or unconsciously. We all know that how a dream is described depends heavily on when it is written down, whether right away or later—dreams written down the same night, as many of my examples were, are of greatest documentary value. When written down later, or retold from memory, conscious ideas play a greater role in the description. But even aside from the fact that it is also interesting to hear how much the waking mind "knew" and supplemented the dream with images from the real environment, these particular dreams about political current events were especially intense, relatively uncomplicated, and less disjointed and erratic than most dreams, since after all they were unambiguously determined. Typically they consisted of a coherent, even dramatic story, and so were easy to remember. And in fact they were remembered—spontaneously, without artificial help—unlike most dreams, especially painful dreams, which are quickly forgotten. (Remembered so well that quite a lot of them were told to me with the same introductory words: "I'll never forget it." And after my first publication on this topic, several people told me dreams that lay ten or twenty years in the past by then, dreams that clearly *were* unforgettable; these retrospective accounts are labeled as such in this book.)

I gathered material in Germany until 1939, when I left the country. Interestingly, the dreams of 1933 and those from later years are remarkably similar. My most revealing examples, however, are from the early, original years of the regime, when it still trod lightly.

Some friends who knew what I was doing helped me, asking around and writing down what they heard. My most important helper was a doctor who had access to a wide range of patients— and he could ask them about their dreams without attracting undue attention. Including the material I obtained second- and thirdhand, I collected dreams from more than three hundred people, so the principles of polling samples would lead to the conclusion that the Third Reich sentenced a very large number of people indeed to similar dreams.

When I received a dream, retold or in writing, I camouflaged my notes or transcriptions as well as I could, for instance replacing "Party" with "family"; calling Hitler, Goering, and Goebbels

Uncle Hans, Uncle Gustav, Uncle Gerhard; writing "flu" instead of "arrest." I hid these bizarre-sounding family stories in the spines of various books in my large library. I didn't have much hope that such pitiful methods would help me if worst came to worst—but what would? Later, I sent the transcriptions to various address in various foreign countries, as letters, where they were waiting for me when I myself had to leave the country.

During the war, I published a small selection of this material in a magazine, as "Dreams under Dictatorship." I was unable to make use of the whole body of material at the time, due to external circumstances.

I'm now glad I didn't compile and discuss my material until a substantial firsthand historical record—facts, documentation, testimony—became available, along with scholarly studies based on it. With its help, I have now been able to try to show psychological reactions and typical behaviors, the immediate effects of total domination on its individual subjects, in a new way: through the documentation of dreams.

I have not included any dreams of physical violence or physiological symptoms of fear, even the most extreme ones. Many dreams began: "I woke up soaked in sweat; yet again, as on so many nights before, I had been shot at, tortured, scalped . . . Blood was streaming down my face, my teeth had been knocked out, I was running for my life with the SA right on my heels." Even among the regime's supporters there were no doubt many who occasionally had such dreams. But there was nothing new about these dreams, except perhaps how common they now were. "Sleep no more! / Macbeth does murder sleep": Tyrants have always done so, violence has always done so, and this was not my area of interest. In every era, we find horrible dreams caused by a collective threat, not just by an isolated threat facing a single person, or from psychological tension within a highly sensitive individual (writers such as Hebbel and Lichtenberg have recorded truly hellish dreams of theirs). Take one such collective situation that is all too common: war. Anxiety dreams from numerous wars have been preserved, but human nature and the expression of human fears remain so similar over time that it is often hard to tell which war they're from, except insofar as the dreams from modern wars overwhelmingly feature modern weapons and the effects of such weapons, since the population as a whole is overwhelmingly vulnerable to them. A dream from World War I symbolizes the dreamer's fears with a frozen prisoner hanging on a pole as starving people rush over to him with knives to carve out the choicest pieces of flesh for their cooking pots, but that same dream might just as well have been dreamed during the Thirty Years' War if it hadn't taken place in a Berlin subway station.

However, even if we didn't know in advance which era the dreams I collected between 1933 and 1939 came from, there could be no doubt about what events underlay them, as widely varied as these dreams are. Their time and place of origin is instantly obvious: They could only have emerged from the paradoxes of life under totalitarianism in the twentieth century, and most of them specifically from Nazi Germany.

Since it is difficult nowadays to narrate dreams without touching on psychological theories, I find it necessary to add the following here: The dreamers in this book are not dealing with conflicts in their private lives, much less conflicts from their past that have left them personally damaged somehow; rather, they are dealing with conflicts caused by a public realm full of stress and agitation from all the half-truths, half-intuitions, facts, rumors, and conjectures floating around in it. These dreams do deal with damaged human relationships, but it is the environment that has damaged them. The "link between dreams and waking life" here in these "transparent pseudo-dreams," to quote Jean Paul, is rooted directly in the political present that the dreamer finds himself or herself in—fertile soil indeed. They are all but waking dreams. What lies behind them is far from invisible—indeed it is all too visible; their surface content is the same as what underlies them. They have no façade concealing personal contexts and associations, and there is no need for anyone else to interpret how events in the dream are related to events in waking life, the dreamer has already done so in the dream itself.

This kind of dream too employs images, but no one needs to explain its symbols, interpret its allegories—at most, we might have to decode some simple ciphers. The dreams make use of disguises and metamorphoses as easy to understand as the ones in satire or political cartoons; the true identity of the person behind the mask is as easily known as in a masquerade ball or carnival.

So such dreams are not prophetic, despite often seeming to be. Their metaphors came true because these dreamers, with sensitivity sharpened by fear and repulsion, perceived almost imperceptible symptoms in the profusion of daily events, and at least in their dreams refrained from charitably explaining them away. The dreams seem a little like mosaics—surrealistically assembled, perhaps—whose individual tesserae are pieces of the reality of the Third Reich. This is what justifies treating them as relevant to the psychology of totalitarian systems, interpreting them with reference to the concrete situations they illuminate and leaving aside whatever references they may contain to the individual dreamer's psychology. (As we know, representatives of more psychological schools of dream interpretation—Bruno Bettelheim, for instance—were astonished to realize how inapplicable their theories were to the most extreme circumstances of the totalitarian state: the concentration camps.)

What we have in these dreams, then, is an unreal reality against the backdrop of a distorted, distorting environment and disintegrating values. The dreams are a blend of logical thought and guesswork; rational details combined into fantastical contexts and thereby made more, not less, coherent; ambiguities that remain ambiguous despite being interpretable; things hidden beneath the surface, or even in unfathomable abysses, brought up into everyday life. This sounds like a description of modern art of all kinds, which should come as no surprise given the role that dreams, even nightmares, have played as artistic devices in the twentieth century. Still, it is nothing short of astounding how closely the expressive means of dreamers in the thirties, exploring their present moment, correspond to the ways that writers today, finding realism inadequate, go about trying to elucidate the past.

It has been claimed often enough that Kafka's parables can be applied to the conditions of life under totalitarianism. In the same sense, we might say of these dreams that they can be applied to the significant results of studies of the Third Reich— not merely as sources of content, but in terms of form. Were someone to publish a selection of the more coherent, dramatic dreams from this book, under a title like *Fragments from Ten Dreamers*, the organized chaos of the dreams, their detailed understanding of external events and psychological processes, would absolutely make the selection qualify as contemporary literature. In struggling to find a way to express the inexpressible, these dreamers blurred the boundary between tragedy and comedy, coming up with parables, parodies, and paradoxes that described the phenomena of the time in only slightly defamiliarized form. They arranged situation after situation in snapshots, in sketches, allowing echoes of daily life to reverberate—eerily loud, eerily soft, radically simplified, radically exaggerated. Whatever the form in which these dreamers, "in slumberings upon the bed," unspooled a thread through the labyrinth of the political present and spun it further even as it threatened to coil around their necks, their power of imagination is impressive.

The Nazi official who remarked that people had a private life under the Third Reich only while they were asleep actually underestimated the dictatorship's powers. The dreamers recorded here, on their way to becoming completely subjected to the regime, saw their situation even more clearly "in a dream, in a vision of the night."

CHAPTER TWO

REMAKING THE INDIVIDUAL, OR "LIFE WITHOUT WALLS"

I will show you fear in a handful of dust.

—T. S. ELIOT

Total domination becomes truly total the moment it closes the iron band of terror on its subjects' private social lives, and it never fails to boast of this achievement.

—HANNAH ARENDT

The most obvious and striking facts of the totalitarian regime—
the rules and regulations, laws and ordinances, prescribed and
pre-planned activities—are the first things to penetrate the
dreams of its subjects. The bureaucratic apparatus of offices and
officeholders is in fact a dream-protagonist par excellence, macabre and grotesque.

One forty-five-year-old doctor had this dream in 1934, a year
into the Third Reich:

> At around nine o'clock, after my workday was done and I
> was about to relax on the sofa with a book on Matthias
> Grünewald, the walls of my room, of my whole apart-
> ment, suddenly disappeared. I looked around in horror
> and saw that none of the apartments as far as the eye could
> see had any walls left. I heard a loudspeaker blare: "Per
> Wall Abolition Decree dated the 17th of this month."

This doctor, deeply troubled by his dream, decided on his
own to write it down the next morning (and consequently had
further dreams that he was being accused of writing down
dreams). He thought further about it and figured out what
minor incident of the day before had prompted his dream,
which was very revealing—as so often, the personal connection
made the historical relevance of the scene depicted in the dream
even clearer. In his words:

> The block warden had come to me to ask why I hadn't hung
> a flag. I reassured him and offered him a glass of liquor, but

to myself I thought: "Not on my four walls . . . not on my four walls." I have never read a book about Grünewald and don't own any, but obviously, like many others, I think of his Isenheim Altar as a symbol for Germany at its purest. All the ingredients of the dream and everything I said were political but I am by no means a political person.

"Life Without Walls"—this dream formulation that universalizes in exemplary fashion the plight of an individual who doesn't want to be part of a collective—could easily be the title not just of this chapter, but of a novel or academic study about life under totalitarianism. And along with capturing perfectly the human condition in a totalitarian world, the doctor's dream went on to express the only way out of a "life without walls": the only way to achieve what would later be called "inner emigration."

> Now that the apartments are totally public, I'm living on the bottom of the sea in order to remain invisible.

An unemployed, liberal, cultured, rather pampered woman of about thirty had a dream in 1933 which, like the doctor's, revealed the existential nature of the totalitarian world:

> The street signs on every corner had been outlawed and posters had been put up in their place, proclaiming in white letters on a black background the twenty words that it was now forbidden to speak. The first word on the list was "Lord"—in English; I must have dreamed it in English, not German, as a precaution. I forgot the other words, or probably never dreamed them at all, except for the last one, which was: "I."

When telling me this dream, she spontaneously added: "In the old days people would have called that a vision."

It's true: A vision is an act of seeing, and this radical dictate, whose first commandment was "Thou shalt not speak the name of the Lord" and whose last forbade saying "I," is an uncannily sharp way of seeing the domain that the twentieth century's totalitarian regimes have occupied—the empty space between the absence of God and the absence of identity. The basic nature of the dialectic between individual and dictatorship is here revealed while cloaked under a parable. This woman herself admitted with a laugh that her "I" was in general quite prominent. But then we have the details that flesh out the dream: the poster that the dreamer put up like Gessler's hat;[1] the outlawed, missing street signs symbolizing people's directionlessness as they are turned into mere cogs. And the simple move of dreaming that the poster listed the English word "Lord," which she never uses in her normal life, in place of the German "*Gott*" serves to show that everything high and noble and excellent is forbidden altogether.

This dreamer produced a whole series of such dreams between April and September of 1933—not variations on the same dream, like the factory owner's, but different ways of processing the same basic theme. While a perfectly normal person in daily life, she proved herself in her dreams to be the equal of Heraclitus's sibyl, whose "voice reached us across a thousand years"— in a few months of dreams she spanned the Thousand-Year Reich of the Nazis, sensing trends, recognizing connections, clarifying obscurities, and vacillating back and forth between easily unmasked realities of everyday life and mysteries lying beneath the visible surface. In short, her dreams distilled the essence of a development which could only lead to public catastrophe and to the loss of her personal world, and expressed it all articulately by moving between tragedy and farce, realism and surrealism. Her dream characters and their actions, their details and nuances, proved to be objectively accurate.

Her second dream, coming not long after the dream of God and Self, dealt with Man and the Devil. Here it is:

> I was sitting in a box at the opera, beautifully dressed, my hair done, wearing a new dress. The opera house was huge, with many, many tiers, and I was enjoying many admiring glances. They were performing my favorite opera, *The Magic Flute*. After the line "That is the devil, certainly," a squad of policemen marched in and headed straight toward me, their footsteps ringing out loud and clear. They had discovered by using some kind of machine that I had thought about Hitler when I heard the word "devil." I looked around at all the dressed-up people in the audience, pleading for help with my eyes, but they all just stared straight ahead, mute and expressionless, with not a single face showing even any pity. Actually, the older gentleman in the box next to mine looked kind and elegant, but when I tried to catch his eye he spat at me.

Like the factory owner, this dreamer understood perfectly the political uses of public humiliation. One guiding theme in this dream, among many other motifs, is the "environment." The concrete stage-setting of the giant curved tiers of seats in an opera house, filled with fellow men and women who merely stare into space "mute and expressionless" when something happens to someone else, very skillfully depicts this abstract concept, with the extra touch of the man who seems from his appearance to be the last person you'd think would be capable of spitting on this young, vain, well-dressed woman. What she called the faces' "mute and expressionless" look, the factory owner had called their "emptiness." (Theodor Haecker, in a dream from 1940, twice mentioned the "impassive faces" of his friends as they just stood and watched him.) Very different people all hit upon the same code for describing a hidden phenomenon of the environment: the atmosphere of total indifference created by environmental pressure and utterly strangling the public sphere.

When asked if she had any idea what the thought-reading machine in her dream was like, the woman answered: "Yes, it was electrical, a maze of wires . . ." She came up with this symbol of psychological and bodily control, of ever-present possible surveillance, of the infiltration of machines into the course of events, at a time when she could not have known about remote-controlled electronic devices, torture by electric shock, or Orwellian Big Brothers—she had her dream fifteen years before *1984* was even published.

In her third dream, which came after she had been shaken by the reports of book burnings—especially the news she'd heard on the radio, which repeated the words "truckloads" and "bonfires" many times—she dreamed:

> I knew that all the books were being picked up and burned. But I didn't want to part with my *Don Carlos*, the old school copy I'd read so much it had fallen apart. So I hid it under our maid's bed. But when the storm troopers[2] came to collect the books, they marched right up to the maid's room, footsteps ringing out loud and clear. [The ringing footsteps and heading straight toward someone were props from her previous dream, and we will encounter them again in many other dreams.] They took the book out from under her bed and threw it onto the back of the truck that was going to the bonfire.
>
> Then I realized that the book I'd hidden wasn't my old copy of *Don Carlos* after all, it was an atlas of some kind. Even so, I stood there feeling terribly guilty and let them throw it onto the truck.

She then spontaneously added: "I'd read in a foreign newspaper that during a performance of *Don Carlos* the crowd had burst into applause at the line 'O give us freedom of thought.' Or was that only a dream too?"

The dreamer here extends the characterization, begun in her opera-house dream, of the new kind of individual created by totalitarianism. But here she includes herself in her critique of the environment, recognizing the typical aspects of her own behavior: The book she tries to hide under a bed like a criminal isn't even a truly forbidden book, only Schiller, and then it turns out she doesn't even hide that—out of fear and caution she hides an atlas, which is to say, a book with no words at all. And even so, despite being innocent, she feels weighed down with guilt.

While this dream gently suggested that the formula Keeping Quiet = A Clear Conscience cannot apply within the new system of moral calculation, her next dream went quite a bit further in that direction. It was a complex dream, with less of a complete plot and harder to understand, but she did understand it.

> I dreamed that the milkman, the gas man, the newspaper vendor, the baker, and the plumber were all standing in a circle around me, holding out bills I owed. I was perfectly calm until I saw the chimney sweep in the circle and was startled. (In our family's secret code, a chimney sweep—*Schornsteinfeger*—was our name for the SS, because of the two S's in the word and the black uniforms.) I was in the middle of the circle, like in the children's game "Black Cook," and they were holding out their bills with arms raised in the well-known salute, shouting in chorus: "There's no question about what you're responsible for."[3]

The woman knew exactly what lay behind the dream psychologically: On the previous day, her tailor's son had showed up in full Nazi uniform to collect on a bill for tailoring work she had just had done. Before the national crisis, of course, bills were sent by mail after an appropriate interval. When she asked him what this was all about, he answered, with some embarrassment, that it didn't mean anything, he just happened to be passing by, and happened by chance to be wearing his uniform. She said, "That's ridiculous," but she did pay. A little piece of daily life—but in these times, ordinary everyday incidents were not just ordinary. The woman used this little story to explain in detail how things were operating under the new "block warden system": the intrusions happening every day and protected by the Party uniform; the many private accounts being settled at the same time; individuals increasingly being encircled by the various little people—Grandpa Tailor, Uncle Shoemaker. All of these figures flitted like phantoms through her Black Cook dream.

The chorus in the dream, though, making her the typical accused person under a totalitarian system with her guilt presumed in advance—"There's no question about what you're responsible for"—is also, in German, a clear reference to Goethe's "All guilt is avenged upon this earth"; it represents her own feelings of guilt at having given in to the pressure despite it being slight pressure, which she called ridiculous and the tailor's son in uniform called just by chance.

Like the *Don Carlos* dream before it, this Black Cook dream describes in a very subtle way the first little compromise, the first minor sin of omission, that snowballs until a person's free will weakens and eventually wastes away altogether. The dream describes normal everyday behavior and the barely perceptible wrongs that people commit, shedding light on a psychological process that even today, despite the best efforts, is extremely hard to explain: the one that makes even those who are technically innocent of crimes guilty.

I would add only that the line about undoubted guilt [*Die Schuld kann nicht bezweifelt werden*] appears in almost identical words in Kafka's story "In the Penal Colony," spoken by the officer: "Guilt is never to be doubted" [*Die Schuld ist immer zweifellos*].

This woman's dreams, full of Orwellian objects and Kafkaesque realizations, tended to repeatedly treat the new circumstances of her environment as static situations: the neighbors with "expressionless faces" sitting around her "in a large circle," she herself feeling "trapped" or "lost." Once—in fact on New Year's Eve, 1933 to 1934, after the customary New Year's Eve ritual of telling fortunes from the shapes made by dropping molten lead into cold water—she dreamed not even situations but pure impressions, words without any images at all. She wrote the words down that night:

> I'm going to hide by covering myself in lead. My tongue is already leaden, locked up in lead. My fear will go away when I'm all lead. I'll lie there without moving, shot full of lead. When they come for me, I'll say: Leaden people can't rise up. Oh no, they'll try to throw me in the water because I've been turned into lead . . .

Here the dream broke off. We could describe this as a normal anxiety dream—there is no pun in German between the metal, "lead," and the verb "to lead" or "a leader"—although it is an unusually poetic one, whose horrors we can feel even without knowing any additional context. (It was used in a short story in 1950.) But the dreamer herself pointed out the scraps of rhyme from the Nazi "Horst Wessel Song" woven into the dream (*geschlossen / erschossen* [locked up / shot full]), and added that she had felt this way, leaden and anxious, for months. If we want to interpret further, we might consider that her phrase "Leaden people can't rise up" uses the verb *aufstehen*, the root of *Aufstand*, "uprising" or "revolution," so the line has a deeper meaning that she didn't see despite being so perceptive otherwise.

In any case, her hiding in lead matches the doctor's hiding at the bottom of the sea as an expression of the wish to withdraw completely from the outside world.

The plethora of prohibitions in early autumn 1933 drove another woman, very different and of different age—a fifty-year-old math teacher—to have the following dream:

> It was forbidden under penalty of death to write down anything to do with math. I took refuge in a bar (never in my life have I been to such a place). Drunks were swaying on their feet, the barmaids were half-naked, the band was cacophonous and deafening. I took an extremely thin sheet of paper out of my bag and wrote down a couple of equations in invisible ink, deathly afraid.

When asked what she thought about this dream, the teacher said only: "They're outlawing something it's impossible to outlaw." Which is perfectly true—and in its perfect simplicity, this prohibition against writing down "$2 \times 2 = 4$," lying outside the bounds of possibility as it does, shows up for what they are all the other prohibitions that strain against impossibility. We can only marvel at the details this relatively unimaginative, conservative schoolteacher managed to drag up out of the secret recesses of her mind: She went looking for a dark and unfamiliar place where no one would expect her, and went to work like an expert spy, with special ink and paper thin enough to swallow, to protect her right to write down equations—her job. In more analytical terms, we could say that she refused to let politics rob her life of meaning, for this dream gives us a new metaphor, from a different angle, for the threat of alienation from one's environment. (We should also note that this math teacher's dream contained one of the very few acts of resistance, no matter how timid, that turned up in any dream by any member of the middle class.)

From this handful of fables about a "life without walls," told in their sleep by a doctor, a pretty young woman, and an older schoolteacher, it is easy to reconstruct the real circumstances that motivated them. Each of them also represents an abstraction (for instance, the woman's "environment dreams" exemplify "the destruction of plurality" as well as the feeling of "loneliness in public spaces" that Hannah Arendt would later characterize as the basic quality of totalitarian subjects). These dreams depict not just environmental shocks but the psychological and moral effects of these shocks within the dreamer's mind.

CHAPTER THREE

BUREAUCRATIC ATROCITY STORIES, OR "I DON'T ENJOY ANYTHING ANYMORE"

We used to have to adjust a few things by hand, but from now on the machine will work all by itself.

—FRANZ KAFKA

What kind of age is this
when a conversation about trees
is almost a crime.

—BERTOLT BRECHT

Self-expression—saying "I don't enjoy anything anymore"—was itself a crime, committed by a man in 1934 Germany, in a dream.

The man, a lawyer and civil servant in the city government, about forty years old, dreamed as follows:

At eight in the evening I was on the phone with my brother—my only close friend or family member. [This was true in real life.] After taking the precaution of praising Hitler for managing everything so well and saying how good everyone in our ethnic community[1] had it, I said: "I don't enjoy anything anymore." [This too corresponded to reality: he had said this on the phone that evening.]

In the middle of the night, the phone rang. A dull, expressionless voice [corresponding to the expressionless faces we have seen in other dreams] said: "This is the Telephone Surveillance Office" and nothing more. I knew at once that my comment about not enjoying anything was my crime. I heard myself begging and pleading to be forgiven this one time, arguing that they could decide not to report me just this once, not pass anything along or hold anything against me. I heard myself pleading my case like a lawyer. The voice remained absolutely silent and then they silently hung up, leaving me agonizingly uncertain.

Even though this civil servant abased himself, like the factory owner in his dream, he was left in the Kafkaesque state of being accused without knowing the accusation—a kind of limbo that is without question a method of systematic terror. A Damocles sword was hanging over his head, but in this case the power that hung it there wasn't Goebbels, it wasn't a specific person at all, but a government office as represented by an impersonal voice. If "enjoying things" is the non-goal-oriented pleasure a person takes in being alive, then the crime of being unable to enjoy anything stands for dehumanization in a world fenced in by ideologies and controlled by a goal-directed dictatorship. This image condenses and expresses the reigning conditions fully as well as the Brecht lines quoted at the start of this chapter, written somewhere else in the world, in exile, at this same period— another exaggeration that only clarifies an absurd reality.

The dreaming lawyer didn't see all this quite as clearly; he saw only that his dream unfolded logically within the framework of his own job. "I dream bureaucratic atrocity stories," he said, using the official term for rumors of terrible misdeeds leaking out to the public.[2] He had invented dozens of offices and departments like the "Telephone Surveillance Office" in his dreams, and had forgotten all of them except the especially catchy "Training Bureau for the Installation of Eavesdropping Devices in Walls." Clearly, his inventions were genuinely surreal, giving "absolute reality" (as André Breton put it) to the reality above reality, the "sur-reality." He had also dreamed up regulations, decrees, and civic associations whose very names sufficed to analyze social conditions, but these too he had forgotten, except for a "Decree Against Interaction with Foreigners" and the brilliantly formulated "Regulation Prohibiting Bourgeois Backsliding Among Municipal Employees."

He remembered, however, that he had seen these names on banners, posters, and page-wide newspaper headlines. Or else, in nonvisual dreams, he had merely heard them, "shouted by a penetrating voice like a drill sergeant's." He mentioned this only in passing, but the mere fact that means of mass communications turned up in this context seems significant. Propaganda is itself an important part of the totalitarian world, and Hitler's regime was the first totalitarian system to make full use of these technological aids to shaping public opinion, just as it made full use of its human functionaries. Both human and nonhuman methods attained a kind of autonomy in this civil servant's dreams, as a new, modern kind of ghosts in the night, behaving exactly as ghosts do: materializing now as an apparition, now as a shout, a voice from above.

As time went on it turned out that propaganda was having an effect as deep as it was supposed to have: The leading role in dreams was very often played by loudspeakers, banners, posters, headlines, the whole arsenal of media in the regime's news monopoly—they appeared so often, and in such similar forms, that we cannot discuss them all individually here (we will see these means of propaganda playing a minor role, however, in the most various kinds of dreams below). Two examples to stand in for the group: One man, who happened to be very sensitive to noise, would dream that he heard his radio blare: "In the name of the Führer . . . In the name of the Führer . . ."—especially after days when a speech of Hitler's had boomed from loudspeakers in houses, offices, restaurants, and on every street corner. In another young woman's dreams, the words "The Public Interest Outweighs Self-Interest" appeared, repeated endlessly, on a fluttering banner—illustrating how deep an effect the mere repetition of the simplest slogans can have.

Others dreamed about slogans and catchphrases distorted or "corrected" as if by a satirist or polemicist. During the real-life public campaign against "grumblers and pessimists" [*Meckerer und Miesmacher*], one man dreamed of a chorus of voices chanting against "crumblers and humblers" [*Muckerer und*

Duckerer, literally "yes-men and cringers"]. Another time, this same person dreamed about the Nazi newspaper *Der Völkische Beobachter* with a headline across the front page that said "Against Faultfinders and Pederasts!"—campaigns had been conducted against both of these. "Is this supposed to be ironic, or modest counter-propaganda?" the dreamer asked himself. One housewife dreamed a slogan—"The Faucet Drips, The Winter Relief Stews" [*Wasserleitung tropft, Winterhilfe eintopft*]—that seemed to criticize the methods of the Winter Relief fundraising in the style of modern rhyming nonsense poetry. (Families were ordered to substitute a simple stew for the usual Sunday roast and turn in the money they thereby saved.) For all its ambiguity, wordplay, and assonance of otherwise unrelated content, there is sense here amid the nonsense.

The details matter less than the fact that all the propaganda media bombarding the dreamers by day were turned into dream-protagonists at night, in a process not so different from the "sleep-teaching" in Aldous Huxley's *Brave New World*, where a device broadcasting the mandated thoughts is installed under a sleeping child's pillow.

CHAPTER FOUR

THE EVERYDAY LIFE OF NIGHTTIME, OR "SO THAT I WOULDN'T UNDERSTAND MYSELF"

For there is nothing covered, that shall not be revealed; neither hid, that shall not be known. Therefore whatsoever ye have spoken in darkness shall be heard in the light; and that which ye have spoken in the ear in closets shall be proclaimed upon the housetops.

—LUKE

There was of course no way of knowing whether you were being watched at any given moment. . . . It was even conceivable that they watched everybody all the time. . . . You had to live—did live, from habit that became instinct—in the assumption that every sound you made was overheard, and, except in darkness, every movement scrutinized.

—GEORGE ORWELL

Propaganda—the means used to manipulate people's minds, from radio broadcasts to newspaper headlines—pursues the subjects of totalitarian rule through their dreams; so too do storm troopers, the means used to impose physical terror, in countless dreams that I will not discuss here since they are so obvious (yet many people dream them nevertheless). However, when a middle-aged housewife dreams that the tiled stove in her living room has become an agent of terror, clearly this is a different kind of terror. Her dream was:

> A storm trooper was standing in front of the large, old-fashioned blue tiled stove in the corner of our living room, where we always sit and talk in the evening. He opened the stove door and it started to talk, in a shrill, penetrating voice [here again we have the penetrating voice recalling the loudspeaker voices of the previous day]. It said everything we'd said against the regime, every joke we'd told. God, I thought, what is it going to say next? All my little comments about Goebbels? But at the same time I realized that one sentence more or less wouldn't make any difference—the fact was, they knew everything we'd thought and said to people we trusted. Just then I remembered that I had always laughed at the idea of the house being bugged; actually, I still don't believe that it is. Even when the storm trooper tied my wrists—he used our dog's leash—and was about to take me in, I thought he was just playing, and I even said in a loud voice: "You can't

be serious, this can't be happening." [This same disbelief in unbelievable reality—this almost schizophrenic split between the person experiencing something and the person looking on—was consistently observed in the concentration camps.]

It is important to realize that this dream of reveries by the Nazi fireside dates from 1933. What today are political facts, everyday realities, were not yet even described in novels: Orwell's ever-present Big Brother did not yet exist, nor did the surveillance and recording devices from the second half of the twentieth century, used without any particular political purpose against a "defenseless society." (The most recent refinement is miniaturizing these devices to the point where they can be installed inside a cocktail olive.) We now also know that the people living under dictatorship were the prototype for the individual in this "defenseless society." But the housewife here, or the civil servant from the last chapter who dreamed about a "Training Bureau for the Installation of Eavesdropping Devices in Walls," didn't know any of that—and yet they did "know" it, precisely as the government wanted them to, and reproduced in the darkness of night a distorted form of what they had already experienced in the dark world of daytime.

The housewife knew what had occasioned this dream—a particularly revealing cause in this case—and included it of her own accord when retelling the dream: "At my dentist's the day before, when we were discussing various rumors, I found myself, despite my skepticism about surveillance, staring at his dental equipment and wondering if there mightn't be some kind of listening device attached to the machine."

We here see someone right in the process of being turned into the victim of a type of terrorization that is difficult to grasp and still not fully understood: the terror arising not from the constant surveillance of millions of people, but from not knowing for sure how complete the surveillance is. Maybe this housewife didn't believe that there really were microphones, but on that day she caught herself thinking that it wasn't totally impossible, and she promptly dreamed the same night that "the fact was, they knew everything we'd thought and said to people we trusted." Could there be any dream better suited to the aims of a totalitarian regime? The Third Reich couldn't install surveillance devices inside everyone's home, but it could certainly take advantage of the fear it installed in the people themselves, driving them to terrorize themselves, as it were. The regime had turned its subjects, without their realizing it, into voluntary collaborators in the systematic terrorization, by making them think it was more systematic than it actually was. This "Dream of the Talking Stove" is, in its way, an example of blurring the line between victim and perpetrator: In any case, it reveals the endless possibilities there are for manipulating people.

The bedside lamp of another housewife soon joined the idyllic storybook nook of the cozy stove in betraying its owner. Instead of bringing light, it brought to light at loudspeaker volume everything she said in bed:

> The lamp was speaking in a loud, shrill voice, like a military officer. At first I thought I would just turn it off and stay safe and sound in the dark. But then I told myself that that wouldn't help. I rushed to see my friend, who owned a dream-interpretation manual, and I looked up "Lamp": the only definition in the book was "Serious illness." It was a big relief, but only for a moment, until I remembered that nowadays, to be safe, people were using "sickness" as a code word for "arrest." Again I felt desperately worried,

at the mercy of that shrill voice that never stopped talking, even though no one was there to arrest me.

A greengrocer dreamed exactly the same thing about the pillow he put on top of the telephone as a precaution when his family was sitting comfortably chatting together in the evenings. The comfort turned to horror when this pillow, which had been embroidered in cross-stitch by his mother—a sentimental memento he kept on his easy chair, his domestic throne—suddenly grew a tongue and started testifying against him, incessantly repeating all the family conversations from the price of vegetables to the midday meal to the sentence: "The fat guy's getting fatter and fatter" [meaning Hermann Goering]. All the while the greengrocer couldn't believe what was happening to him, any more than the housewife by the stove could.

I heard about similarly uncanny household objects many times: mirror, desk, desk clock, Easter egg. In each of these cases, the dreamer didn't remember the whole dream, only that the object was denouncing them. The number of these dreams may have increased as people learned more about the regime's methods. But even these examples from the housewife and the greengrocer, who dreamed about Big Brother's listening ear if not his striking fist—people who also had imposed censorship, tyranny, and terror on themselves during the day, otherwise it would have been hard for them to invent these new domestic tyrants at night—illustrate more than the invisible methods of silencing millions of housewives and greengrocers. They illustrate too the dark shape that these people's "consent" takes. They show how people, in blind fear of the hunter, start to play the hunter themselves, as well as the prey; how they secretly help set and spring the very traps that are meant to catch them.

One dream in this category—grotesque enough to be in a class by itself—came into my hands only recently:

> I dreamed that I woke up in the middle of the night and saw that the two angels hung above my bed were no longer looking up—they were looking down, keeping a sharp eye on me. I was so scared that I crawled under my bed.

Apparently the girl who'd had this dream had had one of the popular reproductions of the putti from the Sistine Chapel above her bed. The dream sounds unremarkable enough, but only at first: She had never realized that these angels stationed to watch over [*wachen über*] her sleep were in fact over-seers, monitoring [*überwachen*] her, and she crawled under her bed as though she had learned from George Orwell that it's impossible to know whether or not you're being watched at any given moment.

With one more turn of the screw, the various precautionary measures taken by day, the disguises and camouflages (also used, of course, in modern art), the bizarre and elaborate rules that private people adopted to try to outwit public rules and laws both real and imagined—these, too, would come to life in dreams. One young woman, who worked as an excellent bibliographer, had this dream:

> I was going to visit a friend, whose name was, let's say, "Klein" [German for *small*]. As I was walking there, I realized I had forgotten her exact address. I went into a phone booth to look it up, but as a precaution I looked up a totally different name, let's say "Gross" [German for *big*], which was obviously pointless. [So said the woman herself, whose job was looking things up!]

This is a literally crazy thing to do, since the action itself defeats the purpose of the action. But it makes so much sense within the craziness of the dreamer's world—it is not at all absurdity for absurdity's sake.

Here is another example, in a single sentence:

> I was telling a forbidden joke, but I was telling it wrong on purpose, so it made no sense.

The same man who dreamed this also dreamed about blind and deaf people he sent out to see and hear forbidden things, so that he could prove whenever he needed to that they hadn't seen or heard anything. He remembered no further details about this obviously farcical procedure.

The most precise example I heard of this kind of dream was from a hatmaker, from the summer of 1933:

> I dreamed that I was talking in my dream and to be safe was speaking Russian. (I don't speak any Russian, and also I never talk in my sleep.) I was speaking Russian so that I wouldn't understand myself and no one else would understand me either, in case I said anything about the government, because that's against the law and would have to be reported.

"Come, let us go down and there confuse their language, that they may not understand one another's speech," it says in the Bible; during the Inquisition, a man was prosecuted for having "spoken heresy in his dream"—the hatmaker surely knew neither of these things. Nevertheless, what she dreamed has since become reality, in Auschwitz, where the impossible became possible: A female prisoner working as a secretary there fearfully asked another woman who slept in the same room if she had said anything in her sleep about what had happened the previous day. "Because we were threatened with punishment if we said a single word about what we'd heard in the political branch, or even conveyed anything with a facial expression." (Quoted from testimony at the Auschwitz trial reported in *Die Welt*.)

A young man had this dream at around the same time:

> I dreamed that I had stopped dreaming about everything except rectangles, triangles, and octagons, which all looked like Christmas cookies somehow. Because we weren't allowed to dream.

Here we have someone who decided to play it safe by dreaming about no physical objects at all.

CHAPTER FIVE

THE NON-HERO, OR "SAID NOT A WORD"

I'm not unjust, but I'm also not courageous.
Today they showed me their world
And I saw only the pointing finger: it was bloody . . .

—BERTOLT BRECHT

He who in any public spot
Dares be depressed will at once be shot;
Showing depression nonverbally
Will be harshly punished equally.

—DREAM-REWRITING OF A STANZA BY HEINRICH
   HEINE, WHICH ACTUALLY RUNS AS FOLLOWS:

He who in any public spot
Ventures to reason will be shot;
Reasoning nonverbally
Will be harshly punished equally.

In Franz Grillparzer's 1834 play *The Dream, A Life,* a dream warns the hero not to assume the burden of any guilt. A century later, in the period covered by the present book, there is a wonderful nonfictional example of someone getting real-life instruction from a dream: The painter George Grosz had a dream in which a friend appeared and urgently advised him to leave for America. Grosz took the advice, and said later that a higher power had saved his life.

But when the dreamer takes an active role instead of a receptive one, stepping out on the stage of the absurdist dreamworld with all its eerie settings, props, and sequences of events we have been following up until now, he or she cannot be instructed and is not wonderful.

We have encountered this active figure already, in bit parts. But since we have to categorize this corpus of dreams to get any kind of overview, I would put the dream-protagonist who defines his own role in the unfolding drama in a different category from the dreamer who simply reacts to what is done to him and to the environment the regime has created around him. The active protagonist plays his part to the point of absurdity and his own depersonalization; he despises himself, curses himself, rubs salt in his own wounds. Above all, he makes himself look ridiculous, carving so much reality out of his self-portrait that what's left is a joke. He also tries to construct alibis and establish a paradoxical innocence, even as his dream deciphers the reality of his life—not concealing it beneath mysterious, hard-to-interpret symbols but dragging it into the light of nighttime darkness, a light that reveals all too clearly its absurdity as well as its horror. Modern literature has taught us the figure of the negative, absurd, macabre, comic hero—the non-hero who performs neither deeds nor misdeeds, merely non-deeds—but anyone who has not yet learned this lesson can study it here at one of the sources. In the present context, the main point is that such dreams straightforwardly express the highly complex reactions and motivations of a conscience that knows more than it is willing to admit by day. (Incidentally, the psychological schools of dream interpretation likewise assume this basic situation of a person confronted by his or her conscience.)

In the following dreams, the world of the Third Reich exists only in the background; front and center we have the person who, in Brecht's words, is not unjust but also not courageous—being shown a world that makes an absolute claim on his conscience as well as his person.

In 1935, a thirty-eight-year-old construction worker had this dream:

> I was at the post office, first in line, by the counter, with a long line of people behind me. The clerk refused to sell me stamps because no one opposed to the system was allowed to buy stamps. Then an Englishman came up—he didn't join the back of the line, he just came right to the front, cutting ahead of me and everyone else—and he told the postal clerk what I should have said to him myself, but didn't dare to: "It's crazy how people are treated in this country, I'll tell everyone about it back in England."

When asked what he thought about this dream, the man said: "I made myself a ridiculous man." (Of course he used the phrase by chance, not alluding to Dostoyevsky's story "Dream of a Ridiculous Man.") He said he had this dream almost every night, at least he thought he did, with additional details and variations that always managed to make the absurd situation even more absurd. One night, only Party members were allowed to buy stamps; another night, only those who supported the regime were even allowed to write letters. In any case, it always turned out that someone else, usually a foreigner, had to express the dreamer's opinion to the person wearing a Nazi uniform, whether a postal clerk, bus driver, bank teller, insurance agent, or simply "the man behind the counter" at the movie theater, soccer game, or anywhere else requiring some official ticket or document for entry. Every time, though, the man dreamed that he was facing his adversary at the front of the line—a "long line of people"—so that it was up to him to say something. He was especially upset that sometimes a woman would be the person who stepped up and said something instead of him; this burly pipefitter felt that the self-caricature in his dream was even more cartoonish when the weaker sex proved stronger.

Indeed, this scene that the man performed with himself at the post office could easily, practically unchanged, be a political cartoon: the long line of people waiting at the counter, all without mouths, and behind the counter a single large mouth wearing the cap and jacket collar of a uniform. It could equally well be performed on stage at a political cabaret, so sharply had the pipefitter spotted and satirically presented the role his humanity was left to play in this new world. But his veiled presentation—that in truth was a brutal unveiling—also raises crucial questions: The image of the long, mute line of people at every counter of public life shows that the prerequisites necessary for someone to exercise their conscience simply did not exist here. Meanwhile his dreams give another succinct allegory for the destruction of pluralism and diversity in the totalitarian state: the prohibition against buying stamps or even writing letters, that is, communicating with others.

A thirty-six-year-old office worker, formerly a member of the Reichsbanner (a pro-democracy paramilitary organization, associated with the Social Democratic Party and fighting both far-left and far-right enemies of the Weimar Republic), had numerous dreams making fun of himself, precisely analogous to the many revealing jokes and popular expressions of the time:

> I dreamed that I ceremoniously sat down at my desk, having finally decided to file a formal complaint against the prevailing circumstances. I put a blank sheet of paper, with not a single word on it, into an envelope and was proud of having made an official complaint, which at the same time made me feel deeply ashamed.
>
> Another time, I called the police department to make a complaint, and said not a word.

For many of us, Weimar Republic comedian Karl Valentin's line will immediately come to mind: "I'm sayin' absolutely nothing—surely we're allowed to say that!" That aside, what a telling picture this is for the universal refusal to speak, and the way that the will to do so is atrophied by constant compromises: When he finally, ceremoniously does decide to act, he no longer can.

Another time, this same office worker had the following dream:

> Goering came to inspect my office in person and gave me a satisfied bow, which I'm afraid made me very happy, even though I was thinking to myself, That fat pig.

By thinking about Goering's comical appearance while guiltily and reluctantly enjoying his praise—the same method as that of the factory owner from Chapter One, who stayed upright only by concentrating on Goebbels's clubfoot—our protagonist here only humiliates himself further.

This hero of two minds about things, both happy and ashamed at his actions—with "two souls in one breast," one of which says no to the environment while the other one says yes—he, too, does not appear in isolation. The circumstances of the time necessarily gave rise to this type of individual, torn between rejection and affirmation, and the following dream paints a precise picture of the complex, complicated feelings he has.

An eye doctor, forty-five years old, in 1934:

> The storm troopers were putting barbed wire into the hospital windows. I had sworn I would never allow them to bring their barbed wire into my ward. But then I did allow it after all; I stood there like a caricature of a doctor as they knocked out the glass and turned my hospital room into a concentration camp with barbed wire—and even so, I lost my job. But I was summoned back to treat Hitler, because I was the only one in the world who could; I was proud of myself for that, and felt so ashamed of my pride that I started crying.

The doctor woke up shattered and exhausted, the way people often are after they've cried in their sleep, and thinking over the dream in the middle of the night he realized what specific incident had given rise to it—again, it is very revealing about the total picture. The previous day, one of his assistants had showed up to work at the hospital wearing a storm trooper's uniform, and although the eye doctor was outraged he had said nothing. He then fell back asleep and dreamed on that same night:

> I was in a concentration camp but all the prisoners were being treated very well—there were dinner parties and

plays being performed. I thought: Well then, so it really is exaggerated, all the things you hear about the camps. Then I saw myself in a mirror: I was wearing the uniform of a concentration camp doctor, with special jackboots that sparkled like diamonds. I leaned against the barbed wire and started crying again.

This doctor himself used the word "caricature" to describe himself, and so indeed he was in these dreams: A cold, clinical pencil has sharply sketched his efforts to reconcile the irreconcilable. In his first dream, he saw the danger of keeping silent: how closely tied doing nothing is to doing wrong. In the second dream, by saying "It's all a lie," he became complicit with the powers he hated: His image in the mirror may have contradicted the self-image he wanted to have, but the jackboots sparkled so seductively. In both dreams, he put himself into a category he didn't want to be in, and while full of shame he was at the same time full of pride at fulfilling his wish to belong (a theme I will discuss at length below).

As for the "barbed wire" that played such a prominent role in both dreams, the doctor himself said that he'd struggled frantically to find the right word in the first dream: Instead of *Stacheldraht* ("barbed wire"), he had first thought *Krachelstaat* (a nonsense word suggesting "decrepit nation"), then *Drachelstaat* (a straight spoonerism), but despite all the Joycean recombinations he couldn't get to *Drachensaat* ("seeds of discord," literally "dragon's seed") which in his opinion he was trying to come up with in order to express what dangerous consequences this barbed wire and these glass shards might have for the visually handicapped.

As everybody knows, the story of the storm troopers and their "night of broken glass" took place in real life years later—Kristallnacht, 1938. One episode occurred with details that almost seem to have been taken from this eye doctor's dream: When the storm troopers broke all the shop windows of Jewish businesses, they also, in a western part of Berlin, broke the windows of a blind man's little shop and then dragged him out of bed and forced him to walk across the broken glass in his nightgown. Here again we see that these dreams remained in the realm of possibility, or rather, of impossibility well on its way to becoming reality.

CHAPTER SIX

THE CHORUS, OR "THERE'S NOTHING WE CAN DO"

I saw the murderers and I saw the victims.
I didn't lack compassion, only courage

—BERTOLT BRECHT

Yes, but that fear is a sideshow. The real fear is being afraid of
the underlying cause of things, and this is a fear that won't
go away.

—FRANZ KAFKA

The doctor who battled the dragon Barbed Wire in his dream hadn't done anything wrong, he had only—to his great distress—failed to do something right. A secretary about thirty years old had likewise done nothing, but something specific was in reality being done to her: She was the product of a mixed marriage, between a Christian man and a Jewish woman, and she had lived with her beloved mother since her father's death. In the winter of 1936–'37, after the race laws were passed and conditions were steadily worsening, she had a series of short dreams very different from one another but all containing the idea of distancing herself from her mother, getting free of her. The law had not only officially made her a "mixed-breed," it had also given her mixed feelings against the one person she was actually close to and was determined never to abandon—rather than making her feel outraged at the law-makers. She was appalled but didn't try to deny these feelings; she brought them up on her own to a doctor who was treating her bronchitis.

Her first dream:

> I was driving into the mountains with Mother. "We're all going to have to live in the mountains before long," my mother said. [At the time, mass deportations still lay far in the future.] "You will, but I won't," I said, hating her and despising myself.

Her second dream:

> I was sitting in a restaurant with Mother under a sign that
> said "Vermin Keep Out." I wanted to make her happy but
> I was suffering unspeakably and hating her as she sat there
> drinking her hot chocolate. [At the time, the "Jews Unwel-
> come" signs had not yet started showing up in restaurants,
> but the dreamer's personal situation made her so clearly
> aware of the problem of so-called "objective enemies" and
> "undesirable" groups that she could predict in detail the
> upcoming campaigns against them.]

Third dream:

> I had to flee with Mother. We ran like crazy. She couldn't
> go on. I put her on my back and kept running. It hurt ter-
> ribly having to carry her. After a long time I realized I was
> undergoing this agony for a dead body. I was overcome
> with a horrific sense of relief.

Fourth dream:

> I dreamed that I'd had a child with an Aryan man and the
> man's mother wanted to take the child away from me
> because I wasn't pure Aryan. I screamed, "Now that my
> mother is dead none of you can hold anything against me!"

It would be inappropriate here (although some will probably
attempt it) to speak of latent, repressed hatred of the mother in
the daughter, a wish for her mother's death existing already and
merely waiting for an outlet applicable to the present—it would
be inappropriate given the real dichotomy of life under the totalitarianism that politics had forced her into. It would be, in
Karl Jaspers's words, "the existential nonsense of dream interpretation" following the "trend of degrading the individual

person." Whether we view these four short dreams in a political or a human context, they show from a new angle what we have already seen: the psychological extremes that can result when the public sphere encroaches on the private realm; how someone can react in their darkest corners when pressure from above makes it too hard to love their neighbor, or even continue to live with their nearest and dearest.

The dream of one twenty-one-year-old student reads like a court transcript in the case of Knowledge v. Conscience. This dreamer had actually done something: In 1935, under pressure from the new race laws and from her family, she broke up with her Jewish boyfriend, a lawyer. She wrote down this dream on the night she had it, explicitly so that she wouldn't forget any details and thereby make things easier for herself. Here it is:

A classroom, very big, almost like an auditorium. I was sitting in the corner all the way to the left in the very back row. Up in front, on a podium, elevated, was the principal of the school: He looked half like my real former principal, half like Hitler. His name was Dictater. It was Race class.

Next to Dictater but at ground level, facing the class, stood Paul (my boyfriend's name) as a teaching aid. Dictater moved his pointer around Paul's face like it was a map. When Dictater asked, "So which facial features of this teaching aid are particularly inferior?" a nondescript old man next to me answered instead of me. He said: "But the gentleman is really quite respectable." (The typical thing that well-meaning people say about people like us; I have heard it many times.) A quiet murmur of agreement in the class. Dictater made a sarcastic face and said (what an exact imitation of professorial irony I came up with here!): "I see, I see. Well, a little while ago this allegedly respectable gentleman expressed to me how displeased he would be about any eventual annexation of Austria."

I realized I had to act fast if I wanted to save Paul, whose touching, deathly pale face I couldn't stop looking at, up there next to Dictater but lower down. I jumped up, ran up the aisle toward the front of the room so that I was standing in the middle of the class, and shouted, "I don't usually say anything" (the typical comment you hear all the time to preface any objection to anything, no matter how slight—why did I say it just then?) "but that's not true, it's not true."

I was counting on hearing an even louder murmur of agreement than before, but instead an icy silence reigned among the benches. Nothing but mute, expressionless faces. Dictater gave a cold, sarcastic smile. I walked a few steps closer to his podium and cried, "Everyone has told me their opinion one-on-one, absolutely everyone. Paul has been treated unfairly and is a good and decent person." Then I added, against my will, since actually I didn't want to say anything critical: "They're not all heroes either, *your* class."

At this a trace of thoughtfulness, of humanity, flitted across Dictater's face up there. But only for a second or two, then he looked icy again. I realized full well— between Dictater's contemptuous face up there, Paul's deathly pale face lower down, and the silent class in the background—that it was a dangerous situation for Paul, but also for me.

Then, right next to the touching, deathly pale face, a blue light came on outside the window, floated slowly through the window, floated toward him, surrounded

him, floated up over Dictater and the class toward me, and
surrounded me too. Then the silenced class found their
voices again. "It's a miracle," they murmured, "a miracle,"
they were almost grumbling. Dictater looked very unsure
of himself all of a sudden.

I too thought for a moment it was a miracle.

Then my friend Eva whispered in my ear in her sharp
little voice: "There's nothing we can do. The light'll last for
a moment then go right out. It's only the funny old lady
who always invites us for a coffee." (In reality the cleaning
woman had turned on the light behind the glass doors to
my room and woken me up.)

What exactly is happening here, in this merciless self-
criticism from someone who knew that the state system had
ruined not only the public sphere but her own particular private
life, forcing her to take a step she didn't want to take? Setting
the dream in a gigantic school auditorium was not a displacement or disguise, for there really were Race classes in the cur-
riculum at the time, complete with living "teaching aids." All she
was doing, like other dreamers, was bringing in a public audience as her nighttime self told a painful personal story—and in
fact, the public belonged there as part of the story. With its mix
of vacillation and action, shame and other personal reactions,
this story contains everything we have already seen in the
non-hero type, and more. Even though the student tries to do
something, she seems to almost insist on showing what she isn't
doing, the kind of person she isn't being. She begins her
resistance by saying "I usually don't say anything"; the man sitting next to her is braver than she is, despite being "old and
nondescript"; she chooses this figure to speak for her, as we
have seen in earlier dreams; we have likewise seen a crowd with

"mute, expressionless faces." She even weaves into her dream how authorities retreat when faced with resistance, like the "blue haze" she is happy to delude herself about until the chorus leader speaks up with the age-old argument: *There's nothing we can do.*

This same student had another dream at around that time, in which she went beyond her "I usually don't say anything" and instinctively made use of her enemy's line of reasoning:

> My boyfriend had decided to ask his assistant to come back to work for him at the office, in spite of the race laws prohibiting it. We drove out to the country—toward Caputh near Potsdam, I think. I dreamed it in color: The pine trees were all gray. I stayed in Paul's car—his little DKW, which is really black, though even that looked dirty gray in the dream—while Paul went up to the house where the trainee lived. The trainee's mother was sitting outside the door with two other women. I expected to see her give an accommodating, somewhat obsequious smile (as she really had once when we'd happened to pass by her place while out for a drive), but instead she started scolding and complaining; it looked like she and the other women were about to start hitting Paul. I wanted to jump out of the car to protect him, to prevent the worst from happening, but instead I heard myself screaming what they, the Nazis, had included as mitigating factors in their race laws: "He went to fight in the war when he was eighteen . . . his father died of a war wound . . . all his brothers were in the war." Meanwhile we slowly backed away. I can't tell you how humiliating and shameful the scene was, I don't think I'll ever forget it.

For several months afterward, this student repeatedly dreamed the following dream:

> People were attacking my boyfriend and I didn't help him, and then he was carried off on a stretcher, with the same "touching, deathly pale face" as in the Race class. But his body was a skeleton, except for one bloody scrap of flesh still hanging from where his neck was.
>
> One time, I said to myself as consolation: "But this is just propaganda, it's an anti-Hitler poster from before." [There had been an antifascist poster in 1932 depicting a skeleton.]

This student's dreams are a good example of the process of inversion at work in propaganda, a process we have already seen in the dream of the doctor who tried to convince himself that there were plays and dinner parties in the concentration camps. She began by using her enemies' arguments "to prevent the worst from happening," and ended up deciding that atrocities were only counterpropaganda. As we all know, propaganda is subject to no legal or moral restraints—it is capable of almost anything and can make events happen whenever it needs them to happen. It can also, however, as we see here in its early beginnings, infiltrate the people it's directed at, until here too the boundaries between propagandist and victim of propaganda gradually dissolve, and suggestion becomes autosuggestion.

CHAPTER SEVEN

IDEAS COME TO LIFE, OR "THE DARK-HAIRED IN THE REICH OF THE BLOND"

It no longer matters whether blue eyes, blond hair, and a six-foot stature truly guarantee superior human qualities. What does matter is that one can use this standard just like any other method to organize people to the point . . . where no one has the chance to think any more about whether the distinction is meaningful or not . . . This apparently minor, in reality decisive operation of taking ideological views seriously . . .

—HANNAH ARENDT

A Nordic soul, a Nordic mind, and Nordic traits of character can only be found in a Nordic body.

—HEINRICH HIMMLER

When, in the imaginary Reich of Dreams, it is no longer the Third Reich's concrete practices that provoke dreams but the all-encompassing fictions (the "theories") the regime is based on—when fantastic doctrines occasion a dream, rather than terror tactics, prohibitions, legal paragraphs, or any other factual basis—then the whole dream becomes a parable of the schizophrenic nature of totalitarian reality. When the theory that the blond race is superior goes looking for nighttime victims with dark hair or other external markers the state has decided are relevant, the resulting dreams are not merely proof that constantly repeated propaganda slogans are effective; they are also a metaphor for everything imaginary, fictive, and artificial in totalitarian reality. (In my experience, the literature on the subject has so far avoided this kind of macabre comedy— genuine black humor.)

A twenty-two-year-old with a delicately shaped but dramatically curved nose dominating her face seemed to believe that everyone thought she was Jewish. Her dreams were soon full of noses and identity papers, papers and noses:

> I went to the Office of Aryan Verification [which doesn't exist under this name, and which she had no real-life involvement with under any name] and handed in a certificate about my grandmother that I had spent months chasing down. The official, who was sitting behind a wall and looked like a marble statue, reached his arm up over the wall, took the certificate, tore it to pieces, and burned

the pieces in a little stove built into the wall. "So, are you still pure Aryan now?"

The door to The Law here is guarded not by Kafka's doorkeeper, "friendly by natural temperament," but by a bureaucrat like a marble statue behind a wall complete with a built-in stove for burning papers. He uses the quite rude "*du*" form of address in speaking to the supplicant, or apparently to anyone without the right grandmother.

In the following months, but still before the race laws went into effect (though they did not apply to this woman in any case), she had a number of long, epic dreams on the theme of noses and identity papers, furnished with numerous elaborate and sometimes realistic details. As in many modern stories, only the starting point of the dream narrative would be unreal.

Another dream about papers:

> Relaxed and peaceful family outing. We were at a restaurant with outdoor tables by the Havel River. Mother and I were carrying some cake in a box and a folder with our genealogy papers. Suddenly there was a scream: They're coming! Everyone there knew who "they" were and what our crime was. Run, run away! I went looking for a high-up hiding place—up in the trees? on top of a cupboard in the restaurant? Suddenly I was lying at the bottom of a big pile of dead bodies, I didn't know how they got there, but at last I'd found a good hiding place. Pure bliss, a sense of salvation, under the pile of corpses with my folder of papers under my arm.

She commented that shortly before her dream she had been deeply struck by a description of the pile of corpses left outside of Khartoum after the Mahdist Revolt. And yet what comes to

mind is that ten years after this dream, during the mass exter-
minations of "the Final Solution," people without the right papers really did have to hide beneath piles of corpses.

She wrote down the following dream about big noses on the
night she had it:

> On the Baltic, on a ship that's swimming with the tide, but
> where it's going nobody knows. [Note that she here uses
> two common idioms in their literal meaning—a Kaf-
> kaesque approach.] Wherever I went, wherever I was, I
> had a giant folder with me that contained my papers,
> because of course I had to prove that despite my nose I
> wasn't Jewish. All of a sudden the papers were gone.
> They're the most important thing, I screamed, absolutely
> the most important thing I have. As I was screaming I real-
> ized that they'd taken them away from me deliberately, the
> ship's officers had methodically taken them and kept them.
> I started looking for them, but quietly, unobtrusively.
> Someone whispered to me: "There's no point, you can't
> do that." [Again the phrase that has come up in so many
> dreams already: "No point . . . you can't . . ."] Suddenly I
> saw my dog, but not as a real live dog, just a ghostly out-
> line. So, they've taken him away from me too—all that
> remained of before when I could relax and enjoy life
> [again, being robbed of happiness by the dictatorship]. I
> burst into tears, a big scene: Fourteen years I'd had that
> dog, for fourteen years I took care of him and loved him
> [an analogy to Hitler's speeches about the fourteen
> shameful years (1919–1933)]. Again someone whispered
> to me that I should control myself and keep my mouth
> shut: Whatever I do, I mustn't attract attention. At that
> point I startled awake. I fell back asleep and the dream

continued: The atmosphere on board the ship got more and more creepy; I didn't dare sit down anywhere and kept asking myself, every step I took, Are they out to get me? Are they staring at me?

Then I was alone with a handsome officer, who was blond—the right type of person, in other words. He came up to me, embarrassed. I asked him about the disappearance of my papers and he looked even more embarrassed: It turned out I was due to be shot. I asked him to let me escape and he said: Not a chance. In desperation I started flirting, trying to kiss him. He said: Too bad, such red lips. Suddenly I realized I was on a Danish ship. We decided that I should swim back to the German coast behind us. So apparently I wanted to go back, despite everything.

I jumped in the water, hid in one of the underwater wooden sheds everywhere, and saw all sorts of Hitler Youth hiking parties go by. I thought how much I wished I could join them.

Back on land I was deeply happy to see German customs-officer uniforms. I was saved. But then I saw my family being thrown overboard—my mother, my grandmother too, my aunt too. What about Uncle, I asked, where's Uncle? "They shot him—they shot all the *nose-suspects*. They're only putting people with non-suspect noses in boats to go to shore." I started crying, I screamed "Uncle!" At the same time I saw the father of a childhood friend of mine reading a farewell letter from his son—this son too had a big nose.

Meanwhile more and more non-suspects were being brought ashore with their belongings. My clothes too, my dresses. Not my papers or my dog. I thought: Ah, that's right, I'm one of the ones who's been shot. Even during the dream I had the thought that I needed to remember this dream.

We could call this dream "A Failed Attempt to Swim with the Tide." Along with all the usual motifs of anxiety and running away, appearing here in contemporary garb, the dream is full of wishes concealed and unconcealed: being torn between the different groups, wanting to belong, wanting to go along with the Nazi movement—all themes we will see again later in the dreams of people who didn't merely imagine they were being "thrown overboard" or "shot."

I was inclined to take this woman with the clearly, specifically racist nose-complex as an isolated case—which would have been interesting on its own—until I came across a whole series of dreams with the same motif from a very different young woman: nineteen, very pretty, but her hair, eyes, and especially skin tone were totally opposite to the blond type. This woman with non-government-approved hair didn't have dreams as frightening as the woman with the government-rejected nose; hers were short sketches, which we might collect under the title "From the Life of the Dark-Haired in the Reich of the Blond." All have as their subject the "inferiority of the dark race." All of the dreams I collected in this category, incidentally, were dreamed by women, usually young women, who perhaps were more sensitive to criticisms of their appearance than men.

First dream-fragment from the dark-haired woman:

> I walked into a store. I looked at the pale-blond, blue-eyed salesgirl, was afraid, and couldn't speak a word. Then I noticed, with a sigh of relief, that at least she had black eyebrows, and I dared to say, "I'd like a pair of stockings, please."

Second dream-fragment:

> I was in a group of people, all blond and blue-eyed, and a
> two-year-old child, who actually can't talk yet, said to me:
> "But *your* kind doesn't belong here."

We see here the ideology of racism, terror, and whipped-up propaganda putting truly amazing ideas into this young woman's head. She constructs a whole everyday world of blonds and populates it with "blond beasts," to use Nietzsche's term—although blond beasts mitigated by black eyebrows, blond baby beastlets . . . It's as if she knew that the only way to parry insanely ridiculous yet murderous ideas was by exaggerating the comedy and insanity. (Not unlike how today's purveyors of black humor show the insanely ridiculous effects of atomic bombs.)

In a third dream, this dark-haired dreamer processed both the dominance of the blonds and the dominance of the group over the individual:

> I was at a sporting event. The audience were split into two
> groups: one blond and blue-eyed, the others with darker
> hair and eyes, the foreigners. [Again foreigners appear as
> the only possible opposing group.] The two groups started
> cursing, jostling, fistfighting. The dark-haired group
> closed ranks and marched away. I marched too, at a slight
> distance, but still in step [so she succeeds in "marching
> with the others"—an idiom for conforming or belong-
> ing]. As I did so, I thought: I may find these people hid-
> eous but I'll put myself under their protection like under
> an umbrella. I really do fall between two stools—I don't
> belong anywhere.

She wanted to belong, though; she dreamed mostly about groups at this point. Here is her fourth dream:

Two passports were sitting on a table, and I had a burning desire to have them so I could be free of this whole thing. I picked them up, but after an inner struggle I put them back down, telling myself: I mustn't do anything that might be held against my group, since all dark-haired people are punished whenever one person breaks the law. [Such group punishments would later prove to be one of the most common measures in the concentration camps.]

In her fifth and last dream, the dark-haired woman grotesquely combined her wish to bear her brunette fate collectively, rather than alone, with the means of expression of a collectivist environment: people speaking in chorus.

I was dreaming that I couldn't talk anymore except in chorus with my group.

"My longing can see only / blond and blue," run the lines by Detlev von Liliencron from thirty years before—just because he was in love with one particular blonde. Now the same tune clearly resounded in countless thousands of heads because there was only one permissible racial type. Readers may well find themselves getting dizzy with all the blond and blue parading before them as we continue, but in this case I cannot avoid the monotonous repetitions. All the stereotyped conflicts between "the dark-haired" and the blonds in these dreams show how the mythologization of one type—not grounded in law and imposed by terror, but merely circulating naturally, supposedly harmlessly—leads to the deviant type, opposed to the natural order of things as it were, adapting and actually feeling like "a lower race." The tyranny of the dominant worldview produced self-tyranny in its victims, as we have seen elsewhere with the tile stove and the pillow denouncing their owners.

Another young woman, who'd been hearing since she was a little girl that she had "raven-black hair," had this dream:

It was Sunday at the Tiergarten Park [in Berlin; *Tiergarten* means "zoo"]. Blond people were out for a walk along all the paths. I heard someone say to the person he was with: "Emma's having trouble with her tenants, they steal like . . ." and I felt deeply ashamed because I thought he was going to say "like people with raven-black hair," and then that's what he did say

Her second dream:

Fritz, who has black hair and dark eyes, was in a fistfight with a blond boy. Even though I knew it was crazy and he couldn't win, even though I knew I felt bad for him, I watched happily, enjoying it. At least he'd tried to defend the black-haired. Eventually he was dead. I've dreamed this many times, with slight variations.

Third:

A blonde, practically still a child, came up to me on the street and asked if I wanted to go out with her that evening. I stared at this nice little teenager in silence: Had she dyed her hair or something? Doesn't she have any racial feeling? What does she really want, what's she aiming at, what are her ulterior motives in talking to someone with black hair?

Even though I hadn't said anything out loud, the blonde answered me: "I'm allowed to invite someone out just because I like them, aren't I?"

Aside from the remarkable inner monologue, this dream contains the surprising moment when the young dreamer "knows" that having nonconformist taste is the criterion for being a non-conforming person, and has a younger person tell her that "just liking them" is a good reason to spend time with someone. When asked what she thought about her dream, the young woman gave an equally surprising answer: "My self-confidence is really low." She also "knew," in other words, that what was fundamentally at issue here was a question of self.

Another young woman with very dark hair had a school dream in which all the dark-haired people formed a group of "Disreputables." She was no doubt recalling her personal experience: The foundation of her complex had been laid in school when she'd been told that she was a member of the Dinaric or Adriatic race and had felt terrible envy of the "first-class" blonds. Here is her dream:

> Little by little the blonds forbade everything to us Dinarics. First we weren't allowed to sit with them. Then we weren't allowed to go out for recess with them. The worst part about it was that the rules weren't being handed down from above, from the teachers, but came from the blond fellow students. Some of them wore badges saying "Non-Dinaric." Finally, when we were huddled around an alcohol stove cooking rice and stewed fruit because we weren't allowed to go out for lunch, the cleaning staff—who acted much nicer than our schoolmates—shared the rumor they'd heard that the worst was about to happen. Without explicitly saying so, they clearly meant that the blonds were going to do us in. The rumor was that an official list had turned up with the names of everyone belonging to the "Disreputables" in every grade. The cause of these measures was also written in the document: We had dared to write a letter to the others, the "reputable"

blonds, over a book we'd loaned them and wanted back. But that wasn't our actual crime, it was that we dark-haired people had written to the blonds at all. Then we all fled for our lives. They threw stones at me.

This "Dream of the Disreputables" adds new details that are insights into the fact that emphasizing natural differences, creating artificial ones, defining elite groups and inhuman groups and then playing one off against the other are basic principles of totalitarian regimes. The dreamer was able to sense these things merely because she had a different skin color and hair color than the portion of the population considered most biologically desirable.

Similar ideas of collective or ethnic guilt filled the heads of other dreamers who had much less fantastical reasons to feel like they belonged to a particular category or were "exponents" of a particular line. A schoolgirl whose father used to be a Communist had this standard dream:

> I get the same grade on every report card, for every piece of schoolwork I turn in: "Very good, but unsatisfactory due to anti-government hostility."

This common nightmare about schools and exams seems to appear with numerous variations among adults (although here it was dreamed while still in school, not years later). I was repeatedly told about dreams where people were told "You'll have to repeat a year because you're a member of the church," or "because you are ideologically unacceptable." Or, posted on a university bulletin board—again, this is practically parody: "So-and-so has failed because he is an enemy of the people." Again the slogans, posters, notices in factories, and so forth had entered into people's dreams.

CHAPTER EIGHT

ACTIVE DOERS, OR "YOU'VE JUST GOT TO DECIDE YOU WANT TO"

Whether or not someone succumbed to the psychological pressure of concentration camp . . . depended almost entirely on their strength of character and whether or not they had a religious, political, or humanitarian sense of purpose.

—EUGEN KOGON

They are driven by their master's empty words, not by their own free will! Protect your property!

—GOETHE

The group that was rather vaguely designated "Disreputables" in the last chapter was specified further, in a dream by a different college student, as the "Suspects." This latter group was not entirely imagined: The dreamer's brother had been arrested and he himself had experienced various difficulties in consequence. Here is his dream:

> There was a dance taking place on every floor of a large building, but we, the "Group of Suspects"—makers of Degenerate Art, former Socialists, relatives of concentration camp prisoners—were sitting in a little attic room, dressed in normal clothes, making fun of all the people arriving in tailcoats and uniforms. I crept downstairs and overheard someone say: "Things are very tense [the German also means: There is high tension or high electrical voltage] in the whole house, and as a result a fire has broken out on the stairs leading up to the attic." I screamed into the bustling crowd, "We have to save the Suspects!" They just shrugged: "Why shouldn't the Suspects go up in flames?"

This student didn't grasp that his "Group of Suspects" clearly represented one of the basic principles of totalitarian rule: that being suspect was a universal fact, whatever the alleged reason, with artists and relatives of those who'd been arrested lumped into the same category. But he did comment: "We Suspects didn't hide in the cellar—we were upstairs, above the ruling class in their uniforms and tailcoats."

This student had felt his brother's arrest as a psychological strain, not just as external pressure: Another of his dreams, for example, was that "It's forbidden to look nervous, and yet I do." All the same, he was proud of his brother, and the thought of his brother's arrest gave him a certain determined resolve. And in fact, he didn't do absurd things in the dream—he took action and tried to save his group.

Another man (I don't know his age or circumstances) showed the same sense of pride when he had this dream:

> All of a sudden I was standing in a column of storm troopers wearing a Red Front [Communist paramilitary group] uniform. I thought to myself: You're in for it now, you must be terribly scared. But I wasn't scared, even when they started tearing my uniform off me and beating me up.

A middle-class housewife had a very similar dream:

> Every night without fail I try to tear the swastika off of the Nazi flag. I'm proud of myself and happy when I do it, but the next day it's always sewn firmly on again.

This dream referred to something that had happened in Berlin police headquarters the day after Hitler seized power: A group of working-class women were waiting to hear news of their arrested husbands, and every time someone walked by carrying a Nazi flag, with its black swastika on a red background, they yelled, "We're gonna rip that off an' it'll be red again!" The housewife who had the dream hadn't been there but had been told about the incident by someone who was. These women's bold determination in the lions' den had made such a deep impression on her that by night she turned into a modern-day Penelope, unweaving for political, not merely personal reasons.

An older woman, a seamstress, who'd had contact with Jehovah's Witnesses and been so influenced by them that she would openly, fearlessly go on and on during fittings about how she refused to swear any oaths or join any organizations, showed the same resolve in her dream, which she described in these words:

> I kept fainting at the corner of the Kaufhaus des Westens [a large department store at a major intersection in Berlin, literally: Shopping Center of the West]. Not a single passerby helped me get up, no one even turned to look at me . . . As I lay there in a swoon I kept frantically trying to figure out how those people knew they had to leave me lying there. How did they know that they weren't allowed to try to help me because I was a believer? They left a human being there on the ground but they picked up a letter I'd been carrying and had dropped—I noticed that once I finally stood up without anyone helping me or caring how unsteady I was on my feet. I felt relieved [literally: I was saved] to see that the person closest to me was a woman in a wheelchair, selling newspapers, so she couldn't have come over to help me anyway.

A woman suspected because of her belief, whom others are forced to leave lying in the street while at the same time keeping everything clean and proper when it came to nonhuman objects; the knowledge that this love of order is itself suspect; the exoneration of the person next to her because she was just as paralyzed as the woman who'd fainted: These images, coming not from an acute intelligence but from an unconflicted spirit, are fully convincing in their purity and clarity.

The stronger a person's power of moral and political resistance was, the more positive, less absurd, their dreams were. I received several dreams from people actively working in the resistance, and they took decisive action in their dreams, too. These stand in direct contrast to the dreams where the protagonist has lost his or her ability to act even while asleep. The wife of a member of the underground—her husband had been discovered but had been able to escape across the border—had this dream in 1934:

He came back, disguised as a soldier . . . Naturally I kept dreaming over and over again that he was back and in danger. "You won't be able to pull it off," I told him, "because you don't know what you're supposed to do." I ran to a barracks to try to steal some printed orders for him—a manual, official instructions; I thought about whether I could sew sergeant's stripes onto his uniform so that rank-and-file soldiers would have to salute him first and he wouldn't be caught giving the wrong salute, because then they'd ask for identification and they'd see that he had false papers. He laughed at my doubts but did his very first salute wrong. I was there and saw him put his hand to his visorless cap totally wrong. Even so, the man he was saluting just froze and stared around in amazement.

Later, I heard that the inevitable had happened: He'd been caught. I kept asking around until I found out where he supposedly was. It was a big cellar, already empty. Everyone had been taken away already. But a group of people who, like me, were looking for someone [what a great group: "people looking for someone"] were living outdoors, near the cellar, sitting in rows of two-seat school desks, and they were talking about only one thing: how terrible it was. When I said "It doesn't look that bad from the outside," they brought me to a little door, actually a trapdoor set into the wall, as round as the lid of a barrel, and it said on it: "Capacity 7.7 cm², Temp. 75°C." I kicked in the lid.

Another time, I dreamed that I was being forced to make a list of every inhuman punishment in the world. I invented them in the dream. [At the time, few details were known about the inhuman atrocities actually occurring.] Then I got even by screaming: "All the enemies need to die!"

The resistance fighter's wife gets even, kicks doors in, steals from barracks—in short, she defends herself and is neither a non-hero nor a non-person. No longer is fear a reason to do nothing.

One very long dream, from 1934, comes from a woman about thirty years old who was in a group producing and distributing an illegal newspaper. She noted the dream down the night she had it, disguising it as much as possible since she was well aware it might be incriminating. It is the longest dream in this book, and action-packed. Justified, well-earned fears have consequences, and every blow is followed by a counterattack.

> I was in a hallway. Five little piles of ten leaflets each had been slipped through the slot in the door; each leaflet had only five words on it. I don't remember what the words were but they very deftly told a whole story: Someone had divulged something, two people had already died as a result, and more would have to die.
>
> At first I was totally calm and thought the whole thing was one of those ads slipped through the door of every house. Then I thought it through further: Each flyer was only a couple of inches large, and not printed. It wasn't even run off on a mimeograph like our newspaper. [She prepared the stencils for this paper, and one day the Gestapo

came by while she was working; this bad scare was what triggered the dream.] The flyers had been made with a child's printing set and so they must have been meant for very few people, probably it was a warning for a small group. Suddenly there weren't five little piles anymore, just one. Like a flash I realized: You can't feel safe anywhere anymore. They were trying to warn me.

My dream was divided into acts, like a play. Once I'd realized, despite my efforts to deny it, that this had to do with me, Act Two opened with me trying to save myself. I went about it logically. First I wanted to put the chain on the door, but that didn't work, the screws had all been unscrewed. Then I realized that it was high time to flee. I peeked out the window and saw figures patrolling down below.

So I had to crawl out on the balcony, which I had camouflaged by painting the geraniums brown, but as I clambered out I thought that it only looked like autumn, not like Nazi. My father came up from the back of the apartment and shouted after me: "You can't do that, it's dangerous." I climbed out without thinking what he said was worth answering. Dangerous? What did he know? (Of course he knew nothing about my underground activities.) I effortlessly climbed from balcony to balcony and even though I was in a hurry I knocked over a couple of swastika flags that were standing rolled up on the balconies as I went.

I landed in the middle of the tables of the café right below the house. I ran inside, into gigantic rooms covered with pictures of Hitler, tearing one of them off the wall as I ran. I tried to think what I should do next—the patrol would be here soon.

Act Three started. I saw two men huddled together in conversation. My brain worked fast and precisely. The whispering men must be talking about something important, I thought. So I went over to eavesdrop on what they were saying. One said: "We need to protest change." (He said "change" as a code word.) The other whispered: "We can't." I pushed my way between them, put a hand on each one's shoulders, and cried: "We've opposed the Party for a long time, we need to protest!" I had two reasons for doing this: First, I wanted to cover my tracks since I was the one the patrols were looking for; second, I figured that if I shouted and ran, the two men would have to run with me. For the cause.

Part Four. They really did run with me, too—half provoked into it, half compromised. I wasn't alone anymore. We ran through the giant rooms (like the Berlin Zoo's pavilions) covered with pictures of Hitler and more pictures of Hitler, running in step without having planned to, as energetically as a person can possibly run. "We've opposed the Party for a long time, we need to protest!" Later, just: "We need to protest!"

People started looking up at us—only a few at first, then more, many approving glances. No one ran with us. We ran down hallways, through more big rooms with Hitler pictures everywhere, and as we ran we cried, "We need to protest!" With incredible focus and all our strength, since we knew that once we'd started we had to keep recruiting more people to run with us or else the game was up, we kept shouting and running, running in step, screaming "We need to protest!" dozens of times, probably a hundred times.

Then I woke up, totally exhausted, and felt compelled to repeat a few more times, in the same rhythm: "We need to protest!" I had to repeat it a few more times during that day.

Here is another dream from the same woman; despite her desperate situation, her dreams seemed quite joyful:

> We were typing stencils for the newspaper. We were discovered. We had to get away. I wanted to bring some money but I didn't have a penny. I started running, with just what I had on me, and someone was chasing me—he looked like a dogcatcher. I thought all my pursuers were dogcatchers, probably to reassure myself.
>
> Down the street, up the next street—finally I got to a little harbor and a boat took me on board. I was relaxed, rowing, it was great. My stencil-making comrades were in the boat too. One said: "Either we stay in the harbor or else we'll have to cross the sea to China and then come back disguised as Chinese people."
>
> Everyone was in favor of risking it. There were three other people in the boat aside from the person who'd spoken up. We all rowed. Suddenly another rowboat stopped us. Again the people with the caps, the dogcatchers—they dragged us onto their boat. The person who'd spoken before whispered to me: "We've got to get weapons." He reached out his hand and took two knives and one fork from a plate that was in our boat: one jagged kitchen knife with bits of the blade missing and one silver knife. He handed out the weapons and I got the silver knife. He stabbed one of the dogcatchers in the back with the kitchen knife. I did the same with my knife, it was horrible, right through his sports shirt. My comrade said, "Sorry." I said, "There's no difference between watching and doing it." The man sank to the floor.

I helped with the next man as a matter of course. We took care of all of them this way, one after the other. Finally there was just one left, the man at the rudder. And he said: "Now that they're all gone, I can say that I was only forced to go along with them. I want to cross the sea with you, take me with you to China." This guy in the cap looked so honest, so scared, that we believed him.

Nowadays we are all too familiar with this type: the guy at the rudder who goes along with it only because he's forced to. His surprising appearance in this context shows how clearly the dreamer herself understood this aspect of the situation.

The same woman had a third dream, depicting in almost unaltered form the shadows the day had cast: Again it was filled to the brim with action and a realistic refusal to give up.

I had crossed the Riesengebirge [literally: Giant Range] mountains on the border to Czechoslovakia on foot, but after only half an hour I suddenly didn't know which way I had come, how I'd gotten there. The only thing I knew was that there were poplar trees there that looked like gallows.

Suddenly I was in Prague. Two comrades were there too, Hilde and Walter. They didn't know the way back either. "Ten days ago I crossed from Krummhübel to Geiergucke with a big pile of material in my backpack," I said, bragging a little, "and three weeks ago I crossed at the Koppe."[1] Anyway, none of us knew the way even though we'd just taken it.

A man in a cap appeared and took my two comrades away. "I'll have you come in later," he said to me. I started to straighten up my bag and figure out what I was going to say.

My name was called. It was a market woman's turn before mine, and there was also a flirty typist there. The market woman had said something but they were letting her go without writing her up. I lashed out. "I've known that gal since I was a child, we went to school together . . ." The man in the cap grinned. "That won't get you anywhere, an SS man hidden behind the balcony (the balcony with geraniums in my apartment) heard everything." I was shocked but I pulled myself together and quickly said, "Then you know all about me, so I guess I can leave now." And they let me leave.

I woke up satisfied with myself, then fell back asleep and dreamed I was in Prague again.

At a cabaret show, suddenly I thought: How am I going to get back? I didn't know the way by foot so I would have to take the train, and for that I'd need a passport. And just then someone came walking through the audience with five or six passports in his hand, which he was giving out to people whose names he called. I grabbed one from him as he walked by. Then a chase—I made it. But when I opened the passport I saw it was an Estonian passport for a twenty-nine-year-old woman, that was okay, but it was covered with stamps saying she had a politically incriminating past. I was still paging through it when I found myself in front of a customs official standing by the train. I smiled and handed him the passport to be stamped. You've just got to decide you want to, I said to myself. And even though he raised his eyebrows at me, I got through.

"We need to protest"; "You've just got to decide you want to"; "I got through"—quite the contrast to the "What could I do?" that we have heard in so many tones of voice throughout these dreams. The conclusions to be drawn from these dreams are no matters of chance or speculation, as we can see from a dream that the student resistance leader Sophie Scholl had in 1943, the night before she was executed. Sitting on her cot, she told her cellmate this:

> It was a sunny day and I was carrying a baby in a long white dress to be baptized. The road to the church ran up a steep mountain. But I held the child tight, safe in my arms. Then suddenly a crevasse opened up right in front of me.[2] I had just enough time to put the child down on the other side, then I fell into the chasm.

Scholl then explained the meaning of this simple dream to her fellow prisoner: "The child is our idea, and it will prevail despite all obstacles. We can prepare the way for it, even though we will have to die for it before its victory."

Here is a transcendent dream, its symbolism shining bright, that the heroes of classical German drama might have dreamed when faced with a classical crisis of conscience.

We can give credit to the dreamers in this category, so unlike the others, for not parodying or degrading themselves, not transcending their real world but not distorting it either. The mirror of their conscience reflected the world clear and undistorted as well.

CHAPTER NINE

VEILED WISHES, OR "DESTINATION: HEIL HITLER"

I saw these men walking back and forth, always the same faces, the same movements; it often seemed to me like there was only one of them. And so this person, or these people, went unchallenged . . .

And I studied, gentlemen, I learned. Oh, yes, you learn when you have to; you learn when you want a way out. You study ruthlessly, you supervise yourself with a whip, you tear yourself to shreds at the slightest resistance.

—FRANZ KAFKA

Marsyas, according to Plutarch, was sentenced to death for having dreamed that he killed the tyrant Dionysius.

I collected only one case of a dream tyrannicide:

> I often dreamed that I was flying over Nuremberg; I had a lasso, and with it I would fish Hitler out of the middle of the Party congress and drop him into the English Channel. Sometimes I kept flying, to England, and told the government—sometimes Churchill himself—where Hitler was now and that I was the one who'd done it.

This modern tyrannicide, beginning with plucking the tyrant from amid his henchmen and followers, was dreamed by a journalist around thirty-five years old. Admittedly, he was free, having emigrated to Prague, and so he was free to dream too. Of course I don't mean that no one in Germany dared to dream about killing Hitler. But although the dreams I collected had so many themes in common that I could derive the typical elements of the various stories in them, the one single dream assassination of Hitler I know of took place abroad. The typical wishes that everyone living under totalitarian rule fulfilled in their dreams looked different. Understandably, they were about collaborating, going along with the crowd, being part of the whole.

The dreams of fear and self-protection we've seen, with their shrugs of "There's nothing we can do, nothing makes a difference," shed light on the psychological process of submitting to *Gleichschaltung*.[1] The vacillations in the veiled-wish fulfillment dreams, in contrast, give us insight into another process, very difficult to reconstruct in hindsight today: how the groundwork for *Gleichschaltung* was laid in receptive individuals even as it was being imposed from without. (Here too, we are dealing not with enthusiastic supporters of the regime, but with people slowly adapting to the new circumstances.)

I collected five of these dreams. Although the situations they describe couldn't be more different, they reveal the same basic psychological pattern, and all end the same way.

The first of these, dreamed by a man in his thirties and written down the same night, runs as follows:

> I had to go collect money for the Nazis at [Berlin's] Zoo Station on Sundays. I thought: Whatever, I want to relax on my day off, I'll bring a comforter and a pillow and no collection box, and just do nothing.
>
> But after an hour Hitler showed up. He was wearing high, shining patent-leather jackboots, like a lion tamer, and crumpled but sparkly purple satin pants like a circus clown.
>
> He went over to a group of children and bent down to them, with fake, exaggerated gestures. Then, in a very different, rigid attitude he turned to a group of teenagers. Then he turned to a circle of spinsterish older ladies, the kind who meet and gossip over coffee, and this time he was flirtatious. (I was apparently trying to express that he was covering all the different groups in the ethnic community [see note 1 to Chapter Three], each with a calculated attitude.)
>
> I began to feel uncomfortable under my blanket; I was afraid he would come up to me as a representative of the "group of people who pretend to be asleep" and realize that I didn't have any collection box. But at the same time,

I was mentally planning the kind of heroic comeback I would have ready for him, something like: I have to be here, but I know about the concentration camps and I'm opposed.

Hitler continued making his rounds. And would you believe it, the other people weren't scared of him at all—one kept his cigarette in his mouth as he talked to him, a lot of them were smiling???

My shift was over, and I took my bed and pillow and went down the large stairway from the station. When I got to the bottom, I looked up. Hitler was standing up there and concluding his appearance by singing an aria from the [nonexistent] opera *Magika* (so many people called what he did "magical"), with extremely exaggerated gestures meant to impress the audience.

Everyone clapped, and he gave a bow and raced down the stairs. Again I noticed his purple circus pants. (I had read the day before that purple was the English color of mourning, so I saw him not just as a clown but in connection with death and grief.)

But where—I looked around—where were his famous bodyguards? He had only a chauffeur in normal clothes with him. He went to the cloakroom like everyone else and waited patiently until it was his turn and the attendant gave him his coat . . . Well, maybe he's not so bad . . . Maybe I'm taking all this trouble to be opposed for nothing.

Suddenly I realized that instead of a pillow and blanket I had a collection box in my hand.

This is like a textbook case of conformity. The dreamer presents agreement as a process, showing at every step of the way both the exertion of influence and the psychological state of the person being influenced. It is as though he were Faust's assistant Wagner and the homunculus in one, with the test tube in his hand that will turn him, too, into a follower. He presents the stages of this process like the panels of a comic strip; he sees through Hitler's methods and Hitler himself, every one of his gestures, with perfect clarity. He sees him as a clown, if a death-bringing clown—and the postwar generation keeps asking, "Didn't our parents see that he looked like a clown?" The dreamer sees Hitler's magical or pseudomagical powers. He sees him as a lion tamer too—and yet the act works; after a while he tells himself that it's not half as bad as it seems, and there's no point in "bothering to be opposed" (precisely the same "*bitt're Müh'n*" or bitter struggle that's the only consequence of bravery in Brecht's *Threepenny Opera*). In other words, he depicts both how we accept external circumstances and the inner state that produces such acceptance: the willingness to let oneself be fooled; the tendency to come up with alibis once we've been conditioned by the right combination of pressure and propaganda for long enough and been made receptive and malleable enough that all our resistance crumbles. (The resistance of Pavlov's dogs collapses too at a certain point; certain specific doses of poison paralyze an organism's defenses; for Orwell's hero in *1984*, too, the moment comes when he looks at a picture of Big Brother with tears of gratitude in his eyes.) This is one side of the coin, the physiological side, but this dream, dreamed by someone neither wholly good nor wholly bad, shows the other side of the coin too: the effects of a social system that allows only one degree of freedom, one direction of movement—toward the "movement."

A young woman at business school, around twenty years old, had a dream that deftly captured a similar situation where "going along with things" was only natural. She dreamed it in 1934, and while it was less detailed than the dream of the man with the collection box, it showed the same process:

> We were celebrating "National Unity Day." [In reality such days were observed, though not under this name; it is very characteristic that she chose this name in her dream.] On a moving train there were long tables in the dining car with long rows of people sitting there. I was sitting alone at a small table. A political song they were singing sounded so funny that I had to laugh. I moved to another table but still had to laugh. Nothing helped; I stood up and was about to leave, then I thought: Maybe if you're singing along it isn't so silly, so I sang along.

Or this dream from the same year, dreamed by an older man; it is so incredibly similar that it highlights the automatic nature of this process:

> I was at a movie theater at Nollendorfplatz [in Berlin], but it looked like an assembly hall. Newsreel. Goering appeared wearing a brown leather vest, firing arrows from a crossbow, which made me laugh out loud (this had actually happened that evening, but nothing had happened to me).
>
> Suddenly, I don't know how, I was standing next to him wearing the same vest and holding the same crossbow, and he made me his bodyguard.

A middle-aged housewife had essentially the same dream in 1936, but with details so close to being realistic that the dream seems almost like a diary entry:

> I was visiting good friends in a little town in Brandenburg— Nauen, I think. That evening there was a party in my

honor, and the next morning we were sitting together eating breakfast and talking over the previous night, in a very warm atmosphere; the dream emphasized how friendly we all were. Then a neighbor walked through the door and she said, without preliminaries: "Last night went on too long and you had too many people over. (Someone had heard this out in the country and told me the sentence word for word, that's probably why I had the whole dream.) And if there were people there who didn't say *Heil Hitler* . . ." I interrupted and cried "Then that wouldn't have mattered at all!" And my friend said: "On the contrary—we would never have had people like that here."

After the neighbor left, my friend tore into me, criticizing me. There was nothing left from the friendship and affection she'd been assuring me of ten minutes earlier. She forced me to leave at once, before anyone found out the truth about me—she literally put me out on the street, without even telling me when the bus was scheduled to come (there was no train). I stood helplessly at the bus stop and didn't understand what was happening, I didn't get how she could switch from one attitude to another so quickly.

When the bus finally came, it was full, and as I got on I said to all the passengers, who were silently staring at me, "*Heil Hitler!*"

Let us summarize what happens in these three dreams. One person tries to laugh at the whole thing, but then sees after a while that she's on a train heading in only one direction; she stops laughing and starts singing along. Another person stops thinking the brown leather vest is funny once he's wearing it himself. And another is ostracized for not saying "Heil," and even while she can't understand how someone "can switch from one attitude to another so quickly," she herself gets on the bus heading in the direction *Heil Hitler*.

Among other things, these dreams show how people who at first thought the whole production was ridiculous (songs, brown shirts, raised arms), who then had no choice but to watch the whole tragic drama of the Third Reich to the end, and who today totally reject it again, with perfect sincerity, can have been the same people all along.

One man managed a dream that captures in a single sentence how undramatic and imperceptible such a transition from suggestion to autosuggestion can be:

I dreamed I said: "I don't *have to* always say No anymore."

This fairy-tale formulation "don't have to anymore"—almost touching amid all the totalitarian versions of "you *do* have to"—shows yet again what a "struggle" it is to be "opposed": Freedom is a burden, unfreedom comes as a relief.

Another man's dream shows the path of becoming a follower from a more direct angle, that of material circumstances:

I walked into a shoe repair shop. "My last pair of soles are all tattered," I said. [There is no pun in German between "soles" and "souls."] The shoemaker replied, holding a brand new pair of shoes, "You know that you can only get new soles if you march with the storm troopers." "I'd heard that," I said, "but I don't believe it." "I can put you into a column where everyone's there only because that's the only way they can get new soles," he said, in a friendly voice. "You'll get two pairs of soles on the spot when you join." Then he added, sounding even friendlier,

"Why don't I give you three pairs right now, because we need you."

I ran away, but as I ran my tattered soles fell off my feet.

This dream was told to me thirdhand by a shoemaker, in these exact words. A customer had told it to him, saying it was his brother-in-law's dream, and had then said: "Not six months later he joined the SA and became a storm trooper."

CHAPTER TEN

UNDISGUISED WISHES, OR "HE'S THE MAN WE WANT WITH US"

I could never have achieved this if I'd been stubbornly set on clinging to my origins, my childhood memories. In fact, the highest law I imposed upon myself was to give up being stubborn.

I was told later that I made remarkably little noise, from which they concluded that either I would die soon or, if I managed to survive the critical first phase, I would be very amenable to training.

I survived.

—FRANZ KAFKA

Dreams that openly, with childish directness, express the wish to join and to belong—as opposed to revealing this hidden wish gradually, step by step, through a slowly developing plot— are surely like the tens of thousands, hundreds of thousands of daydreams people have on the way from opposition to conformity when the path of resistance proves too stony.

This category of dream tends to follow a fixed pattern, endlessly repeated and far less imaginative than the other types of dream we've seen. I collected not just one or two but dozens of these matching dreams, from people of various ages and social positions. What we've seen as a secondary motif in earlier dreams—being an advisor or friend to Hitler, Goering, or Goebbels—is here the main topic. The dreamer childishly exaggerates his or her personality and status, rather than satirically distorting it: "I'm Hitler's right-hand man and I'm happy about it." Dreams like this, which can be summed up in a simple, one-sentence wish, are typical of children, who have not yet learned how complicated adult wishes can be.

Yet some of these dreams were a bit more complicated. Here is one from a twenty-six-year-old transportation worker:

> I was marching along in a storm troopers' procession, but not in uniform. They wanted to beat me up, but then Hitler came up and said: "Leave him alone, he's just the man we want with us."

And one from a sixty-year-old man:

> I was standing on the curb and I saw the Hitler Youth
> march by. They surrounded me and shouted in chorus:
> "Be our troop leader!"

There is, of course, no doubt as to the prominent role of
women in the Third Reich, but it must be said that the genre
of women's wish-fulfillment dreams confirms everything
claimed or suspected in this regard. I will give a half dozen
examples of these dreams, with explicitly erotic components—
they may be monotonous and very much like one another,
but the reader should take them as showing the typical aspects of this mechanism. The connection between power and
sexuality is of course nothing new—power is erotic—but in
this case its effects were felt from the beginning, in the pro-
Hitler voting patterns of women. And the effect was calcu-
lated. "It's got to be a bachelor, then we'll get the women"[1]:
This was decided before Hitler became the Führer, and as we
know he kept faithful to this plan until just before his death,
although not beyond it.

One older woman, who assured me that she was "against
anything erotic and against Hitler," told me:

> I often dream about Hitler and Goering. He wants some-
> thing from me, and I don't say "But I'm a respectable
> woman," instead I say "But I'm not a Nazi," and that makes
> him like me even more.

A thirty-three-year-old housemaid dreamed:

> I went to the movies. The theater was very big and very
> dark. I was scared, I wasn't actually allowed to be there,
> only Party members were allowed to go. Then Hitler came

and I was even more scared. But he not only let me stay, he sat down next to me and put his arm around me.

A young salesgirl:

Goering was trying to feel me up at the movies. I said, "But I'm not even in the Party." He said, "I don't care."

Another salesgirl:

I was at a concert. Hitler walked along the front rows, shaking hands with everybody. Can I hold out my hand for him? I feverishly wondered. Don't I need to tell him that I'm opposed? Meanwhile he got to me and took my hands in both of his hands [a typical Hitler gesture conveying special intensity of feeling; she must have often seen photographs of it]. He continued to hold them until I woke up.

A housewife:

As I'm coming back home from shopping, I see that there's going to be dancing in the streets—like on Bastille Day in France—because it's a holiday to commemorate the Reichstag Fire. Bonfires[2] everywhere [what a brilliant directorial piece of parody!]. Square areas had been roped off and couples were ducking under the ropes like boxers getting into the ring . . . I thought that was hideous. Then someone grabbed me from behind with his strong hands and pulled me through the ropes onto the dance floor. When we started dancing I realized it was Hitler, and thought that was very nice.

More unambiguous situations were no doubt dreamed just as often, but not reported; I didn't ask about it, since it didn't matter for my purposes. That detail is irrelevant here, compared to the basic situation of the Führer as, in effect, a seducer, the object of an erotic wish. The following dream, from another housewife, shows most clearly the blending of the sexual and the political spheres:

> There were long tables on the Kurfürstendamm [a main boulevard in Berlin], and people dressed in brown were sitting packed tight at the tables. I was curious and sat down too, but off to one side, at the end of an empty, isolated table. [She uses an image very much like that of the woman in the dining car dream.]
>
> Then Hitler appeared, romantically dressed in a tailcoat, with a big bundle of fliers that he handed out in a hurry, not paying any attention to who he was giving them to. In fact he just tossed a bundle onto the end of each table, and the people sitting there passed them around. It looked like I wasn't going to get any, but then he suddenly placed a bundle carefully down in front of me, totally unlike what he'd been doing.
>
> Then he handed me a single flyer, while with his other hand he stroked my hair and then stroked farther down my back.

Here the left hand knows exactly what the right hand is doing, as the saying goes: One of them distributes propaganda while the other one caresses. It's impossible to imagine a more concise and trenchant description of Hitler's influence on large swaths of women.

Even more significant are the wish-fulfillment dreams of people whose wishes cannot possibly be fulfilled, due to insurmountable objective, not psychological, obstacles—not some wrong opinion, say, but a wrong kind of grandmother. In short, they couldn't ever fulfill their wishes except at night.

One young woman with a Jewish grandmother had this dream in 1935, right after the race laws had turned her into a newly minted "25% mixed-breed":

> At Bad Gastein [a spa]. Hitler was taking me down a big, sweeping outdoor flight of stairs, visible from a long way off, while carrying on a lively conversation with me. Down below was a spa concert and a crowd of people, and I was proud and happy as I thought: Now everyone can see that our Führer doesn't mind being seen in public with me, despite my grandmother Recha.

Likewise soon after the race laws, a forty-five-year-old woman and "50% mixed-breed" had this dream:

> I was on a ship with Hitler. The first thing I said to him was: "Actually I'm not supposed to be here. I have some Jewish blood." He looked very nice, not at all like he usually does, with a round, pleasant, kind face.
>
> I whispered in his ear: "You know, you could be really great if you acted like Mussolini, without this stupid Jewish business. It's true that there are some very bad people among the Jews, but they're not all criminals, you really can't say that." Hitler listened calmly and seemed very sympathetic to everything I was saying.
>
> Suddenly I was in another part of the ship full of SS men in black uniforms. They were nudging each other, pointing to me, and telling each other in tones of the highest respect: "Look, that's the lady who told the big guy how things really are."

So much for this half-Jewish woman's dream (incidentally, she told it to her tenant unasked and with apparent satisfaction). It shows in miniature how willing people were to submit to Gleichschaltung even if they didn't qualify for it: She merely had "some Jewish blood," was generally speaking against Jews, spoke familiarly to Hitler [using the "*du*" form], told him how he could be "really great," and the SS had "the highest respect" for her—all in one short dream.

So-called "full Jews"[3] seem to have had this kind of direct wish-fulfillment dream only rarely, not because they were unwilling—naturally they would have reacted like any other segment of the population—but because their circumstances were such that even a dream couldn't make them fit the story (further proof of how precisely these dreams reflected the reality of the public sphere). The mother of a fifteen-year-old Jewish boy told me that he had dreamed he was marching with a Hitler Youth group; he was standing "at the side of the road, burning with envy," and then sudden he was "right in the middle of them."

One Jewish doctor's wish-fulfillment dream had a very different emphasis: "I cured Hitler," he dreamed (although this was an aside in the dream, not the main topic)—"I was the only person in the Reich who could," just like the anti-Nazi eye doctor in Chapter Five. The main theme of the dream went like this:

> "What do you want in exchange for curing me?" Hitler asked. "No money," I said. Then a tall blond man from Hitler's entourage said: "What, you crooked Jew, no money?!" And Hitler commanded: "Of course no money. Our German Jews aren't like that."

The doctor had several variations of this dream. In one, he responded to the man insulting him by saying, "If I wasn't German, if I was American or English, you wouldn't dare say that"; another time, he wanted Hitler to reinstate him as a German.

Aside from wishes such as these, which as I've said seem to have been quite rare, the dreams of Jews in the Third Reich occupied the same realm of fear and opposition as the dreams of all the other groups, but within this realm they represented a separate category, just as they themselves were a different category under the Nazi regime—the target of open, not latent, terrorization from the beginning. For this reason, I have decided to discuss the dreams of Jews in a separate chapter.

CHAPTER ELEVEN

JEWISH DREAMERS, OR "I'LL MAKE WAY FOR THE TRASH IF NEEDED"

It's not possible to drive out all the lice and all the Jews in a single year, of course—it has to happen over the course of time.

—HANS FRANK, GOVERNOR GENERAL OF
OCCUPIED POLAND

The *Untermensch* is a mere attempt at a human being, having humanlike facial features but being intellectually and spiritually lower than animals . . . Within such a person there is a gruesome chaos of wild, unrestrained passions: a nameless destructive urge, incredibly primitive cravings, and undisguised beastliness.

—PROCLAMATION OF THE REICHSFÜHRER SS,
HEINRICH HIMMLER

As I've mentioned, it would be possible to tell from the previous chapters' dreams *when* and *where* they were dreamed even if we didn't know already. The first three dreams in this chapter also clearly tell us *who* dreamed them: They can only have been assimilated Jews under the Third Reich. All three of these dreamers were lawyers—perfectly assimilated types in attitude, appearance, and behavior, and too old for their set ways to possibly be reshaped now. The dreams' subject is the displacement, disorientation, depersonalization, and loss of identity and continuity we have seen so much of, but to an extreme that reflects how the dreamers experienced these forces in reality.

The first, a Berlin lawyer and notary public in his early fifties, had an insignia showing that he had seen frontline service in World War One, and so he had been allowed to keep his job even under the new race laws. In 1935, he dreamed:

> I was going to a concert, and I had a ticket, or at least I thought I had one. It turned out that it was only an advertisement, and someone totally different was sitting in my seat. A lot of other people were in the same situation. As we all slowly filed out of the auditorium down the center aisle, heads bowed, the orchestra started intoning "We have no abiding home here."[1]

The second man, about five years older, had the following dream after the exception for veterans had been canceled and he'd lost his job:

I was going to the Justice Department, elegantly dressed in my best suit (as I had actually done thirty years before—it was customary after you'd passed your assessor's exam). The Justice Minister was sitting behind a gigantic desk (like the one we all know from photographs of Hitler), surrounded by SS guards; he was wearing a kind of cross between a black uniform and a lawyer's robe. (I probably had this dream because I'd had to throw out my lawyer's robe the day before.)

I told the minister: "I am filing a complaint that the ground is being pulled out from under me." The guards grabbed me and threw me to the floor. As I lay there, I said: "I even kiss the ground you're throwing me down on."

The third lawyer, five years older still—around sixty—was man in whose life the idea of "proper bourgeois appearance and reputation" had always been very important. His dream, from around the same time, carries the hair-raising, grotesque *J'accuse* of the second dream another logical step farther:

There were two benches in the Tiergarten Park, one a normal green bench and the other painted yellow. [Jews were allowed to sit on only the yellow benches at the time.] There was a trash can between them. I sat on the trash can and hung a sign around my neck, the kind blind beggars sometimes have, which the authorities also make "race defilers" wear. The sign said: "I'll make way for the trash if needed."

These three dreams, each in their own fashion, tell the story of how a long life's foundations are destroyed—like the math teacher's dream in Chapter Two, where it was forbidden on penalty of death to write down anything to do with math. But these dreams emerged so directly from the actual reality the dreamers were subject to that they have no surrealistic quality: The first two border on kitsch, or at least sentimental pathos, as tragedy often does, while in the third, long before Beckett put his characters in trash cans in *Endgame*, the dreamer sat himself on one, in the endgame of his own life as it were, and was even ready to move aside still further to make room for the trash.

The "Dreams of the Three Assimilated Jews" interpret themselves. Rather than comment superfluously, perhaps I might say a few words about what became of these dreamers. I haven't received any news about the second, the one who still kissed the German soil. The first, after he did lose his "abiding home," was able to go abroad and find his footing—he may have been no longer young, but he was not yet old. The third, too, escaped abroad, but died there, a broken man, willing as always to "make way for trash."

A young woman, Jewish, baptized as a child and very German-looking, had a dream in 1934 that provides something like a theory of the dreams of people who had been rudely awakened from the dream of assimilation. In the form of a dramatic speech, her dream makes clear—clearer than our analysis—what can happen in the minds of people who thought they belonged to a society when that society is de facto reorganized to exclude them. It shows us the details of this bloodless drama that heralded the bloody one. She dreamed:

> I was taking a walk in Switzerland with two blond navy officers. A large, very ugly Jewish woman slowly sank to the ground in front of a shop window. Her husband rushed over and said, "Rosa, what's wrong?"
>
> Only when they walked off past us, clutching each other tight, could we truly see how Jewish and ugly they

were. I could feel my two companions shudder with disgust. They didn't say anything, but I did, blurting out: "They're hideous to me too, I can't stand the look in their eyes. But you've forced me into company with them, literally beat me into being one of them. I'm still not one of them, though. But you? What do I have in common with you? You, who look like me—I look like them, like you—what's that got to do with me? At most that I might go to bed with one of you . . ." Then I woke up and wrote down my outburst word for word. [It needs no interpretation or commentary; at most, we might point out that she displaced even this inner psychological turmoil to another country, as a precaution.]

Even if, as we've already seen, people from all segments of the population could recognize the goals and principles of the totalitarian state from the beginning, and could extend them, mapping out their consequences, to the point where their fears look prophetic in retrospect, the sensitivity of the Jewish people was so sharpened by the acute threat they were under that their precisely naturalistic images of the situation seem downright clairvoyant. One thirty-five-year-old housewife dreamed, in 1935:

> While we were taking a walk we heard a rumor on the street that we shouldn't go back to our homes, something was going to happen. We stood on the opposite side of the street and peered longingly up at our apartment: The blinds were shut, it looked uninhabited.
>
> We went to my mother-in-law's apartment, our last refuge at this point. We went up the stairs, but there were totally different people living there now. Had we gone to the wrong building?

We went up the stairs of the building next door, but that was wrong too, it was a hotel. We left by another exit and tried to find our way back, but now the whole street was impossible to find.

Suddenly we thought: There's the building we need so badly. But again it was the same hotel that had fooled us before. As we were repeating this nerve-wracking run-around a third time, the woman who owned the hotel told us: "Even if you find the apartment, it won't make a difference. What's going to happen is this:" And she declaimed, in the form and with the gestures of Christ cursing Ahasuerus [who thereby became "the Wandering Jew"]:

It is a law:
They shall dwell nowhere.
Their fate shall be
To wander the streets.

She returned to prose and intoned in a flat voice, as if reading a proclamation out loud: "Taking effect simultaneously with the abovesaid law, everything that is still allowed shall be forbidden, to wit, entering a store, employing craftsmen . . ." And in the middle of this horror a minor point popped into my head: Where was I going to go to get my new suit made?

We left the hotel and went out into the gloomy rain *forever* . . .

This woman—not herself Jewish, but married to a Jewish man and so bound up with the fate of the group—anticipated by several years the gradually encroaching events to come, from the running-around of those in hiding during the "Final Solution" to the minor details that make life difficult. She even captured the formal mix of bureaucratese and pathos that Nazi proclamations often had: a linguistic reflection of their true nature.

Another man, a lawyer, gave the curse on the Wandering Jew a new twist in this 1935 dream, in which he wandered on foot to "the last country in the world where Jews are still tolerated":

> That was what the country was called—it didn't have any other name. It was located at the end of the earth. My wife, my old blind mother, and I were trudging secretly through snow and ice; we had to cross Lapland, and Lapland wouldn't let us through. But suddenly all that was behind us and the sun shone bright before us on the green grass of "the last country where Jews are tolerated."
>
> A smiling customs official, rosy-cheeked like a little marzipan pig, gave a polite bow and said: "May I help you, sir?" I showed him my passport and said: "I'm Dr.—— ..." [a title used in German by professionals with any advanced degree]. "You're a Jew!" he screamed, and he threw my passport back onto the Lapland ice.

Again one is reminded of Brecht, who wrote: "Fleeing my countrymen . . . / way up in Lapland / heading for the Arctic Ocean / I see one little door left."

This Jewish lawyer came up with the same image in his dream as the fleeing poet, but took it a step further: Even the last remaining little door was slammed in his face. He discovered the worldwide version of exile and exclusion even as he remained in the land of his birth, where he encountered new forms of exile and exclusion every day.

During a present that was difficult enough, dreamers anticipated the difficulties, great and small, of the future—the never-ending questions of where to go, what to do next. Many Jews' dreams were filled with these questions, which I will only summarize, partly because many of their details are hard to understand today without their specific historical context, and are only partly relevant to the goal of this book; partly because, however horrifying they were, they cannot help but pale in the light of the horrors that were to come later. The most fantastical things happened in these dreams with passports, visas, and documents. Dreamers were not allowed across borders, not allowed to dock or disembark, their ships wandered aimlessly around on the ocean. If they did arrive somewhere, they were unwanted guests at friends' houses, they didn't dare join their hosts at the table, they slept eight to a room and worked as maids or servants, they were scared of dark walls and bare courtyards, they would hear a German song and feel ashamed that it moved them, they mispronounced everything and people laughed at them. In short, they failed to find the identity they'd lost. These dreams describe in astounding detail the characteristics of the forced emigrant, no longer young, misunderstanding and rejecting the strange new environment and unable to get over debilitating homesickness—a state that many of these emigrants couldn't endure, even if they reached the foreign country alive.

One example is the dream of a Berlin housewife in her early thirties, full of rules and exemptions, prohibitions, and discriminatory measures that follow her across the Atlantic. It dates from 1936:

> After a long journey I arrived in New York. But you were allowed to stay there only if you climbed up the outside of a skyscraper. The only exception was if you'd been baptized; people said about that group: "The little Nazis are so nice and dependable." Here too the same distinctions between different groups.

I never knew which direction to go in and always got lost. I thought, My poor husband, this is just how he always pictured it.

Suddenly I was on a narrow road, hilly, with watches, bracelets, and other jewelry lying out in the snow to either side. I wanted badly to take some, but didn't dare to, thinking it had surely been left there by the "Foreigner Honesty Validation Office" and they'd probably deport anyone who tried to take anything. Or maybe I was just on a road that was totally forbidden anyway and I was going to be deported no matter what?

I couldn't find the entrance to the language school, then I couldn't find a seat. I was the only one left standing while everyone else sat in their proper places. I didn't have the book the others were all reading and didn't even know what it was called. Even at the entrance to the school I'd immediately thought it looked old and ugly, back home they're much nicer. [This "back home" was so typical of the emigrants that many countries referred to them as "the *chez nous.*"]

Then we were asked to give our age. "Do we have to say?" I asked. "Yes, you have to," the teacher said. I said: "Back home no one *has to do* anything."

I looked out the window, crying. The landscape looked like back in Brandenburg and I started to feel a little better, then the teacher said: "The little Nazis don't only look respectable, they're the only respectable people of any of you."

Along with dreams projecting fear and self-protection into the future, I came across many variations of a new motif: the fear of losing one's mother tongue.

One man made a Trappist monastery "somewhere in the world" the eerie scene of this anxiety: "Everyone who could no longer speak anyway had taken refuge in its gloomy old stone halls and cells."

Another got lost in the desert and found water that you could drink only if you read out loud from a book in the "desert language." He refused, saying: "I'd rather die of thirst than speak that foreign desert language."

And another, who was supposed to translate something into French before being allowed to enter Morocco, refused as well: "It's not worth it," he said, "you can't stay where you end up anyway." At which point he started singing in German: "Oh valleys wide, oh mountains high . . ."

German poems and songs wandered in many forms through these dreams. They were dreams of a lost homeland even though the dreamers still found themselves geographically in the country they'd already lost. One twenty-seven-year-old woman sang the following song in her dream:

> Now Olly's got it good
> She's landed in Hollywood . . .
>> [The first line of a hit song from before Hitler's time]
> There you'd find your peace . . .
> At last stillness would fall . . .
>> [Two lines from well-known lieder]
> It'll all come again someday . . .
>> [A line from a popular song]

She also incessantly dreamed about singing a line from Friedrich Rückert's poem "From My Youth": "When the heart is empty, when the heart is empty, when the heart is empty . . ."

One time, her dream reworked the whole stanza: Instead of the original's

> The swallows return, the swallows return,
> The empty box swells again.
> When the heart is empty, when the heart is empty,
> It will never be full again.

the lines ran like this [both versions rhyme in the German]:

> The swallows return, the swallows return,
> The empty box grows heavy.
> If your heart is empty, if your heart is empty,
> Then you will never return.

This too is prophetic in retrospect—most of those who left, so heavy of heart, longed to return, but few did. In the framework of this book, the dream-rewriting is as logical as that of Heine's poem in the epigraph to Chapter Five.

A Berlin bank employee, about forty years old and fired for being Jewish, dreamed in 1936 that he had emigrated, was doing well in the new country, was working at a bank again, was getting ahead, and could afford his first vacation trip to the mountains:

> I went mountain climbing with a guide [in German the same word as "leader": *Führer*]. And then, on the highest peak, it happened. The guide / *Führer* threw off his cape and hood and stood revealed before me in full SA storm trooper uniform.

He dreamed about rebuilding his destroyed identity, but only to set up the anticlimax of the dream: Despite his successful climb in his new circumstances, the forces that were out to destroy him and which he failed to recognize in time in their new guise accompanied him and suddenly stood revealed before him on the mountaintop as the "*Führer.*"

Precisely matching this dream from 1936—the same way we have seen so many dreams in this book resembling one another—is the following, from the winter of 1960. It was dreamed by a woman who was still a child during the period our other dreams come from.

I saw a heap of letters in the foyer. They were addressed to me and almost every one of them had been opened. One of them—the envelope open and the letter sitting outside it—was still damp and limp from the steam. I thought: Don't modern letter openers have more scientific methods? and I started to complain to the doorman who was standing there.

Next to him there was another man, short and thin and nondescript, in some kind of black suit and with meticulously parted hair. Yes, he said, quite right, I've come on account of your letter situation. That sounded good. Great, I said, and I was about to explain to him what had happened.

He interrupted me: "Show me your ID." I said: "You can't be serious, everyone in the building knows me, I've lived here for years, and the doorman . . ." He cut me off: "Your papers!"

He stood up straight, growing taller and taller, and his suit was no longer just any black suit, it was *the* black suit, with insignia gleaming and sparkling on it.

"No," I said; he had no right to ask me for my ID unless he showed me a warrant. I was the one who had a complaint to make. "And I'm a free citizen."

He slapped me in the face—left cheek, right cheek—and repeated: "Papers." I said no, no, and then he said: "Unnecessary anyway. We know you and know who you are and what you are," and he hit me again. Then he grabbed my wrists and tied them with the chain from the elevator.

I said softly and sadly, mostly to myself, "I'd hoped I would recognize your kind right away the next time you came. I guess it's my fault I didn't."

Then I started screaming, clinging like any normal person to the desperate hope that someone would hear me and come help. But I *knew* that no one would come anymore, ever again.

As mentioned, this dreamer is from a generation linked neither by fear nor by guilt to the past of the Third Reich. Her fear is directed at the present (she had this dream a few hours after hearing an alarming political speech), and she feels it is cause for guilt if we fail to recognize this century's public phenomena that threaten us until their insignia visibly gleam and sparkle. That is the moral of her fable.

That is also the moral of all the political fables dreamed under the Third Reich. Like all fables, they contain not only a lesson but a warning: that totalitarian phenomena need to be recognized for what they are before they throw off their cape and hood, as in the mountaineering dream; before we are no longer able to say "I," but have to speak so that not even we can understand ourselves—before the "life without walls" begins.

NOTES

Chapter One: How This Book Came to Be

1. Tr.: In the original: his attempt at *Gleichschaltung*. Literally "synchronizing," in the sense of "coordinating by force" or "imposing mandatory conformity," this was the Nazi term for the imposition of total political and social control—turning labor unions into Nazi organizations, putting pressure on civic associations, universities, and other institutions to expel Jewish members, and so on.

2. Tr.: Quoted in his *New York Times* obituary, October 23, 1965, p. 31.

3. Tr.: In German, "diary" is *Tagebuch* or "daybook"; Beradt coins the corresponding word *Nachtbuch* or "nightbook."

Chapter Two: Remaking the Individual, or "Life Without Walls"

1. Tr.: Idiom meaning something that exists to compel a public display of subservience. In the story of William Tell, Gessler, the legendary bailiff of the village of Altdorf, put his hat on a pole in the market square and every passerby was required to stop and bow to the hat. William Tell refused, and so was sentenced to shoot an apple off his son's head.

2. Tr.: This somewhat more general term is used throughout the book to refer to "members of the SA."

3. Tr.: In this game, children form a circle and one child runs around the outside of the circle, singing a song about "the black cook from America" (or in some variants from Africa), "marching around and then getting your head chopped off," etc. When the running child taps a child in the circle, they start running around the circle together; the last child left standing is the black cook. What the chorus says rests on the fact that *Schuld* in German means both "guilt" and "debt": "There's no doubting your *Schuld*" means both "what you owe" and "the fact that you're guilty."

Chapter Three: Bureaucratic Atrocity Stories, or "I Don't Enjoy Anything Anymore"

1. Tr.: *Volksgemeinschaft*: a Nazi-era term, literally "people's community," but given an explicitly racist meaning.

2. Tr.: *Greuelmärchen*, literally "fairy tales of horror," a word that implicitly casts the rumors as childish lies.

Chapter Eight: Active Doers, or "You've Just Got to Decide You Want To"

1. Tr.: From Karpacz in Poland to the Výrovka mountain in Czechia, and at the Kopa, another mountain peak on the border.

2. [C. B.:] The symbol of the steep hill and the abyss is familiar from other famous political dreams, for example, Madame Jullien's during the French Revolution and one of Bismarck's dreams.

Chapter Nine: Veiled Wishes, or "Destination: Heil Hitler"

1. Tr.: See note 1 to Chapter One, above.

Chapter Ten: Undisguised Wishes, or "He's the Man We Want with Us"

1. Tr.: Remark attributed to Nazi writer Dietrich Eckart.

2. Tr.: In German *Freudenfeuer*, literally "fires of joy."

3. Tr.: *Volljuden*, the Nazi terminology for someone with either three or four Jewish grandparents.

Chapter Eleven: Jewish Dreamers, or "I'll Make Way for the Trash If Needed"

1. Tr.: From Brahms's *Deutsches Requiem*.

INDEX

A NOTE ON THE TYPE

This book has been composed in Arno, an Old-style serif typeface in the classic Venetian tradition, designed by Robert Slimbach at Adobe.